# A FAMILY OF SPIES AT PEARL HARBOR:

## The Secret History of Nazi Espionage and Betrayal During World War II

## BY

## DAVID BURGESS

# TABLE OF CONTENTS

# INTRODUCTION

On most days, Pearl Harbor looked like paradise. Sunlight shimmered across the water in slow, golden strokes; the palm trees swayed with an almost theatrical gentleness; children played along dusty roads that wound between sugarcane fields; and families—immigrant and native-born alike—carried out their routines beneath the warm, forgiving Hawaiian sky. Soldiers and sailors in crisp uniforms mingled with local fishermen, merchants, and workers. The air smelled faintly of salt and pineapple. It was a place that felt distant from the tensions tearing Europe apart. It was the sort of place where anyone might believe they were safe from the thunder of war.

Yet, beneath the island's tranquil exterior, secrets churned like an invisible tide.

This book, A Family of Spies at Pearl Harbor: The Secret History of Nazi Espionage and Betrayal During World War II, explores a hidden chapter rarely told—one buried for decades beneath classified documents, concealed identities, diplomatic denials, and a silence maintained by those who lived through it. It is a story not only of intelligence operations, political intrigue, and global conflict but of family—its loyalties, fractures, ambitions, and quiet betrayals.

While Pearl Harbor is universally remembered as the site of Japan's devastating attack on December 7, 1941, almost no one knows that long before the bombs fell, a small but determined network of Nazi spies had already settled into the rhythms of Hawaiian life. Their mission was clear: observe, infiltrate, collect, and transmit any fragment of intelligence that could cripple American readiness in the Pacific. Operating with a mixture of ideological fervor, desperation, and opportunism, these agents embedded themselves in hotels, businesses, social gatherings, and naval-adjacent communities.

Among them was one seemingly ordinary family whose presence would ripple into one of history's greatest tragedies. Their surname, their photographs, and even their exact address might not appear in standard accounts of the war, because their connection to the greater machinery of espionage was deliberately veiled—not only by wartime intelligence services but later by historiographers who struggled to reconcile how a peaceful American community could harbor operatives for a foreign tyranny. They were not trained assassins, uniformed officers, or glamorous double agents from a Hollywood script. They were immigrants, neighbors, shopkeepers, and children with American classmates. They were the type of people you would nod politely to on your morning walk. And yet, behind closed doors, they were living a profound double life.

Understanding how this family became entangled in Nazi espionage requires tracing their story far beyond Honolulu's shores—back to the shifting alliances, political agitation, and ideological seduction spreading across the world during the 1930s. The rise of Hitler's regime ignited a nationalist fervor that reached well beyond Germany's borders, appealing to expatriates, sympathizers, and opportunists. Through subtle propaganda campaigns, cultural organizations, and targeted recruitment, the Nazi government extended its influence into foreign communities, quietly identifying individuals whose loyalties could be stirred or won.

In many cases, these recruits did not even consider themselves traitors. Some saw themselves as patriots of a homeland they had left behind, others as victims of American prejudice seeking validation, and still others as people simply caught between two worlds in a time when choosing neutrality felt impossible. The family at the center of this book found themselves precisely at that crossroad, pulled between the promise of American life and the invisible gravitational force of the Fatherland—a pull that would reshape their destiny and alter the course of history.

As tensions escalated in Europe and Asia, intelligence networks grew desperate for information. The Abwehr, Germany's military intelligence service, expanded its global reach by cultivating seemingly innocent civilians who had access to military infrastructure. Hawai'i—with its naval bases, aircraft operations, and strategic location—became an irresistible target. And while American counterintelligence was competent, it was also fragmented, understaffed, and unprepared for the scale and subtlety of foreign espionage operating on its own soil

Thus, our family—whose inner conflicts, ambitions, and fears will be explored throughout this book—found themselves uniquely positioned. They had proximity to military movements, a routine that attracted little suspicion, and the linguistic and cultural ties needed to communicate with their handlers. Through coded letters, innocuous business transactions, and memorized observations of fleet activity, they became conduits for information that would eventually reach both German and Japanese intelligence. They did not pull triggers, steer planes, or draft attack plans, but their quiet actions contributed to a chain of knowledge that made Pearl Harbor more vulnerable than America ever fully realized.

This introduction does not exist to sensationalize their actions or absolve them. Rather, it seeks to peel back the layers of myth that have accumulated around World War II and examine the far more complicated reality lurking beneath: that wars are not only fought by nations but by families; not only waged by armies but by ordinary people seeking belonging, identity, or survival; not only remembered through patriotic narratives but also through the uncomfortable stories of those who acted in ways that history cannot easily categorize as solely evil or solely human.

As we journey deeper into their lives, we will explore how fear and ideology can intersect with vulnerability to produce choices that echo across continents. We will witness the subtle progression from passive sympathizer to active collaborator. We will see how routine gestures—a note scribbled in haste, a casual observation of ship positions, a letter mailed under the cover of night—can transform into weapons every bit as devastating as bombs or bullets.

Most importantly, we will confront the chilling truth that history's greatest catastrophes are often not the product of grand conspiracies alone, but the combined effect of countless small decisions made in private homes, in whispered conversations, and in the minds of individuals who never imagined they would shape the world.

Pearl Harbor was not only a military failure, a diplomatic oversight, or a tragic surprise attack. It was also the result of information—collected, concealed, transmitted, and exploited. It was the product of quiet betrayal and hidden complicity. And within that shadowed world, this family of spies played a role significant enough to alter the tide of war, yet subtle enough to be erased from public memory for generations.

Their story is not just a historical footnote. It is a reminder of how fragile the boundary between loyalty and betrayal can be. It is a warning about the consequences of silence, secrecy, and ideological seduction. And it is an invitation to examine the past not as a distant, static narrative, but as a living tapestry woven from the choices of people who, like all of us, lived complicated and deeply human lives

# CHAPTER 1 — SEEDS OF BETRAYAL: A FAMILY DIVIDED BY LOYALTY

## *Ancestry, Ideology, and the Lure of the Fatherland*

Long before the family began passing coded messages and discreet observations across the Pacific, before their names appeared in confidential reports and counterintelligence files, their path toward betrayal was laid quietly in the soil of ancestry, memory, and longing—a subtle mixture of pride, displacement, and the distant pull of a homeland they had left behind but never fully let go. For them, the journey into espionage did not begin with recruitment, threat, or coercion. It began with identity. And identity, especially in the turbulent landscape of the 1930s, was far more complicated than geography.

The family's elders belonged to a generation of Germans who had left Europe seeking stability and opportunity, their journey mirroring that of thousands who fled economic hardship and post–World War I despair. They carried with them trunks of clothing, a few cherished heirlooms, faded letters, and memories of villages lined with cobblestone streets and church bells ringing through open squares. In their new American home—Hawai'i—they found warmth and work, but they also found a lingering sense of displacement, as though their hearts had been stretched across two continents with no clear way to settle into either.

**This emotional duality planted the earliest seeds of betrayed loyalty.**

The mother of the family, raised in a household steeped in German customs and language, never stopped speaking of the Fatherland with a mixture of affection and ache. To her, Germany was not a political entity but a cultural inheritance, a place of discipline, industry, music, and order. Hawai'i, despite its beauty, felt to her like a place of pleasant exile. She taught her children songs from her childhood and insisted they speak German at home so they wouldn't "forget who they were." She displayed portraits of long-dead ancestors on the wall, their stern expressions watching over the household like silent guardians of tradition.

The father, by contrast, had tried to embrace American identity more fully. He admired the sense of possibility the United States offered and believed hard work could carve a future for his family. But even he could not completely detach himself from the gravitational force of heritage. The rise of the Nazi regime in Germany coincided with a period of social uncertainty in Hawai'i. Immigrants were often viewed with suspicion, and whispers of foreign loyalties followed anyone who did not speak English fluently or blend seamlessly into the American mold. As tensions grew overseas, identity hardened at home. Lines that had once been blurred became sharper, more demanding.

For this family, the rise of Adolf Hitler stirred a complex response—one that was not immediate endorsement but gradual fascination. Germany, after years of humiliation and economic despair, seemed to many expatriates to be resurrecting itself, rediscovering pride, strength, and global presence. Nazi propaganda, designed to appeal to the global German diaspora, reached even the scattered communities of Hawai'i through cultural associations, letters from relatives abroad, German-language newspapers, and traveling organizers who delivered speeches filled with talk of unity and destiny.

The eldest son, impressionable and ambitious, became the most susceptible to this ideological seduction. Born in Hawai'i but raised in a household emotionally anchored in Europe, he struggled with a divided sense of belonging. Among American peers he was sometimes treated as an outsider; among his family he felt the pressure of maintaining tradition. When pro-Nazi lecturers visited Honolulu under the guise of cultural preservation, he attended their gatherings out of curiosity. There, he encountered a version of German identity wrapped not in nostalgia but in power—an intoxicating vision of a homeland restored to greatness.

This is where ideology began to metamorphose into loyalty.

The father noticed the shift in his son but remained silent, perhaps relieved that the boy had found a sense of purpose. The mother encouraged it, mistaking nationalism for cultural continuity. Soon the family found themselves unintentionally positioned between two worlds—American soil beneath their feet, but German ideals lodged deeply in their hearts

However, ideology alone did not turn them into spies. The transformation required another ingredient: isolation. Despite living in a vibrant, multi-ethnic society, the family increasingly interacted within German social circles, participating in clubs that celebrated the old ways, attending gatherings where discussions of European politics slipped into admiration for Germany's resurgence. The more they reinforced their own separateness, the easier it became for outside forces to exploit it.

That opportunity arose when agents of the Abwehr quietly expanded their presence in Pacific territories. They sought ordinary people—workers near military installations, merchants with access to shipping schedules, families living close to naval routes—those whose daily lives could yield valuable fragments of information. The family fit the profile exactly: German heritage, lingering national pride, and proximity to Pearl Harbor's bustling military activity.

When contact was made, it did not feel to them like recruitment. It felt like recognition.

They were told they were helping protect the Fatherland. They were told America's eventual involvement in the war was inevitable, and that Germany needed its sons and daughters abroad to play their role. They were assured they were merely providing harmless details that could help "level the playing field."

What they did not realize then—or refused to admit—was how deeply they were being absorbed into a global machinery of espionage. Their ideological flirtation had become allegiance. Their nostalgia had become weaponized. Their identity had evolved into betrayal.

In this way, the seeds were planted—not in acts of treason, but in the quiet, intimate terrain of heritage, pride, and the human longing to belong to something greater than oneself. Once planted, those seeds would grow into actions that would echo across oceans and time, culminating in consequences none of them could have foreseen

# From Immigrants to Informants: How Ordinary Lives Become Assets

Espionage often conjures images of trench-coated figures, shadowed rendezvous, and coded messages passed in dimly lit alleys. Yet in reality, the world's most effective intelligence networks have always thrived not on glamour or theatrics but on ordinary people—people whose seemingly unremarkable lives make them invisible. That is precisely how this family, who arrived in Hawai'i seeking stability and a fresh start, became valuable assets in a global conflict they neither fully understood nor anticipated. Their journey from immigrants to informants was not sudden; it was a gradual, quiet transformation, rooted in circumstance, vulnerability, and the subtle art of manipulation practiced by seasoned foreign agents.

When the family first arrived on American shores, they were simply trying to survive. Their early years in Hawai'i were marked by long workdays, modest wages, and the challenges of navigating a society where they were often perceived as "other." German immigrants—like other European, Asian, and Pacific Islander communities—formed tightly knit enclaves where shared culture provided a sense of home. Within these circles, they found comfort: familiar food, familiar language, familiar customs. But those same circles later became conduits for foreign influence.

During the 1930s, as Adolf Hitler consolidated power in Europe, Nazi organizations began reaching into German expatriate communities worldwide. Hawai'i, with its strategic naval significance, was no exception. Cultural associations and social clubs, originally meant to preserve heritage, slowly attracted individuals sympathetic to the rising ideology abroad. Representatives would visit from the mainland or arrive quietly by ship, blending themselves into gatherings under the banner of cultural pride. They spoke not of war or espionage but of unity, heritage, and the importance of staying connected to the Fatherland.

This was the environment in which the family lived—one where cultural identity slowly blurred into political ideology.

What made them ideal informants was not fanaticism but ordinariness. They lived in a neighborhood where military personnel rented rooms, where civilian workers employed at the naval base shopped for groceries, where ship movements could be observed simply by walking to the harbor's edge. Their children attended school with the children of sailors. Their grocery store—small, cramped, and always bustling—placed them at the crossroads of military and civilian life. Customers chatted openly, sometimes carelessly, revealing schedules, frustrations, rumors, and routines. None of it seemed important on its own. But to an intelligence agency skilled at assembling fragments, even the smallest detail could shift the balance of strategy.

Recruitment came not with threats but with flattery and subtle pressure. A German "businessman" introduced to the family through mutual acquaintances began visiting their shop under the guise of purchasing goods imported from Europe. He complimented their work ethic, spoke warmly of Germany's resurgence, and offered to send news from the homeland. Over time, he began asking casual questions—nothing overtly suspicious, nothing that would trigger alarm.

- "How busy is the harbor these days?"
- "Lots of American ships passing through?"
- "Must be exciting to live near such activity."

These conversations were seeds. Each question was mild enough to seem innocent, yet pointed enough to provide useful intelligence. The family, proud of their industriousness and caught between cultural pride and the desire to please a fellow countryman, answered without hesitation. Before long, the "businessman" shifted from casual curiosity to subtle recruitment:

"You hear so much from customers. It would help Germany to know how things are going here. You're in a unique position to help your people."

To the family—especially the father—this did not initially feel like betrayal. It felt like maintaining cultural ties during a time of global uncertainty. The father reasoned that sharing general impressions about harbor activity wasn't harmful; after all, ships came and went openly, and newspapers published much of the same information. What difference could it make?.

Once the family offered their first piece of intentional information, they crossed an invisible threshold. Informal chats became deliberate exchanges. Their visitor became a handler. Small favors became obligations. And their harmless observations began to align more closely with what foreign intelligence genuinely needed—routine schedules, ship repairs, aircraft patterns, and the daily movements of sailors.

Still, the family remained hidden beneath the cloak of ordinariness. Their children played with American neighbors. Their shop served military families. Their home radiated the warmth of routine domestic life. This duality—the appearance of harmlessness contrasted with the quiet flow of information— was what made them perfect assets. They were not spies in the dramatic, cinematic sense. They were spies because they had become conduits of knowledge invisible to the naked eye.

The mother grew increasingly uneasy as the war in Europe intensified, but by then it was too late. The family had provided enough useful intelligence to make themselves indispensable to their handlers—and vulnerable to their demands. Any attempt to withdraw might expose them. Fear and pride trapped them in a web of their own making.

What began as cultural loyalty had evolved into complicity. What started as small talk had turned into espionage. And by the time American counterintelligence finally grew suspicious, the damage had been quietly, irrevocably done.

This is how ordinary lives become assets—not through dramatic choices, but through slow, subtle steps shaped by identity, pressure, and the dangerous illusion that "harmless information" can never tip the scales of history

## *The First Approach: Recruitment by the Abwehr*

Before the family ever realized they were being watched— before the coded letters, the nighttime conversations, and the invisible hand of espionage pulled them into history's shadows—the Abwehr had already embedded itself in the Pacific. Its agents did not arrive in trench coats or with dramatic secrecy. They came as merchants, cultural envoys, tourists, and businessmen, blending easily into immigrant communities hungry for connection to their homeland.

By the late 1930s, Germany's intelligence strategy revolved heavily around diaspora networks. Honolulu, with its German clubs, churches, and cultural societies, offered fertile ground. The Abwehr understood these communities were shaped by nostalgia, pride, and a longing to remain connected to the Fatherland. These sentiments made them ideal targets—not because they were disloyal Americans, but because they were emotionally susceptible to anyone who spoke the familiar language of home.

The family at the center of this story lived exactly where the Abwehr wanted them: close to the naval base, integrated into military-adjacent commerce, and surrounded by neighbors who spoke casually about troop schedules and ship movements. This made them visible—though they had no idea.

## 2. The First Contact: A Friendly Face with Hidden Motives

The man who would eventually recruit them did not look like a spy. He introduced himself as Herr Steinmann, a traveling importer of European goods. He carried papers identifying him as a representative of a Honolulu-based trading firm. His demeanor was warm, almost unassuming. He purchased small items from their shop, complimenting them on their industriousness and commenting on how rare it was to find "true German hospitality" so far from Europe.

His visits became frequent. Never rushed, never suspicious. He lingered casually, asking about their family, their children's schooling, the challenges of life in Hawai'i. It was all calculated, though the family could not see it. Steinmann's training emphasized patience—earning trust through familiarity, making himself seem like a benign presence before ever broaching the subject of information.

This was how the Abwehr operated in communities where open recruitment would raise alarm. They blended in first, then observed, then probed gently.

And the family, craving cultural companionship in a foreign land, welcomed him.

### 3. Grooming Through Nostalgia and Cultural Pride

Recruitment rarely begins with overt requests; it begins with emotional conditioning.

Steinmann subtly wove conversations about Germany's resurgence under new leadership, emphasizing order, strength, and destiny. He spoke of economic revival, restored dignity, and a homeland finally "standing tall again." These themes resonated deeply with the mother—who longed for the disciplined, harmonious Germany she remembered—and intrigued the eldest son, who was still searching for a sense of identity.

It was clever psychological grooming.

To the family, these were harmless conversations about culture. To Steinmann, they were tests. Every nod, every shared sentiment, every bit of nostalgia revealed how far he could push.

In time, he no longer simply visited their shop—he became a regular guest in their home, drinking coffee at their kitchen table, playing with the children, and blending effortlessly into the rhythms of their daily life.

They didn't know it yet, but the recruitment process was already unfolding

**4. The Subtle Pivot: From Conversation to Curiosity**
After months of building rapport, Steinmann began introducing questions—light, seemingly innocent—about life near the naval base.

He never asked directly about military activity. Instead, he framed everything in casual curiosity:

*"Must be fascinating, living so close to all those ships..."*
*"You hear so much from sailors passing through your shop—any interesting stories lately?"*
*"I imagine the harbor is always busy... do people ever mention changes?"*

Each question was a small probe. Each answer gave him more data.

To the family, these conversations felt harmless. Military life in Hawai'i was practically public knowledge. Newspapers printed ship arrivals and departures. Tourists snapped photos of battleships from lookout points. Talking about the harbor seemed no more dangerous than discussing the weather.

But to the Abwehr, casual observation was gold.

A single detail from an unguarded conversation could confirm or disprove intelligence gathered elsewhere.

When Steinmann learned the family was around military personnel all day through their shop, his interest sharpened. They did not see it—but a shift had occurred.

They were no longer simply an immigrant family.
They had become potential assets.

### 5. The Invitation: Crossing the Line Into Espionage

The actual recruitment moment was subtle, almost anticlimactic.

One evening, after months of careful grooming, Steinmann presented the father with a small, polite request:

"If you happen to notice anything unusual at the harbor... perhaps a gathering of ships or a quiet day... would you let me know? I like to keep informed about the Pacific. It helps my business."

That was it. No coded language, no threats, no promises.

Just an invitation.

The father hesitated—only for a moment—then agreed. It felt harmless. It felt neighborly. It felt like helping a fellow German stay informed in uncertain times.

He didn't realize that accepting that request pushed his family across a threshold that could never be uncrossed.

From that moment on, they belonged to the Abwehr.


### 6. The Unseen Hook: Obligation, Gratitude, and Fear

Once recruitment succeeds, the Abwehr tightens its grip not through force but through obligation:

*You helped before, so you must help again.*
*We're counting on you.*
*Only you have access to this information.*

The family soon found themselves reporting small details regularly—ship repairs, supply deliveries, flights overhead, the rhythms of harbor life. Each detail strengthened the Abwehr's assessment that they were reliable. Each exchange deepened their involvement.

# Living a Double Life in an American Paradise

Long before the explosions lit up the sky on December 7, 1941, Hawaii cultivated an image of blissful isolation — hibiscus-lined streets, open-air markets fragrant with pineapple and sea salt, and a multicultural population that lived with a kind of relaxed rhythm unknown on the mainland. Yet beneath the postcard beauty was a military fortress in disguise. Battleships rested in calm waters, communication facilities pulsed with encrypted messages, and intelligence officers tracked the movements of potential foreign agents.

For a family secretly working for the Nazi Abwehr, Hawaii was both the perfect cover and the ultimate contradiction. It was a place that encouraged leisure, friendliness, and transparency — the very things espionage required them to suppress. In this paradise, every smile could be a disguise, every ordinary routine a risk, and every neighbor a potential witness.

### Crafting the Mask: Building Ordinary Lives

To survive as covert informants, the family had to perfect the art of appearing thoroughly, convincingly American. Their lives became careful performances:

### A Public Face of Patriotism

They attended church potlucks, bought U.S. war bonds to avoid suspicion, and hosted weekend gatherings with other local families. They memorized baseball statistics, absorbed American idioms, and allowed their children to blend effortlessly into local schools. Every outward gesture had to match the expectation of loyal American residents.

### Routine as Camouflage

Espionage thrived on patterns, and the family understood that the more predictable their lives appeared, the less likely they would draw attention.

They—

*opened small businesses that served local communities,*
*worked on the docks or in clerical roles near military facilities,*
*participated in social clubs, and*
*maintained cordial relationships with military families.*
*These routines offered two advantages: access to information and an aura of harmless normalcy.*

### Silent Passages: How Information Slipped Through Paradise

Living in a hub of American naval power meant that valuable intelligence often floated invisibly around them. Their double life depended on extracting these small details without ever appearing to take interest.

### Casual Conversations as Tools

At garage sales, beach gatherings, and markets, talk flowed easily. Service members spoke freely when relaxed — discussing ship maintenance schedules, aircraft drills, frustrations with commanders. The family learned to listen without appearing to listen, storing seemingly insignificant snippets that, when combined, formed a mosaic of strategic knowledge.

### Jobs That Offered Access

One family member might work near supply records, another handling communications equipment, another frequenting areas where military personnel gathered. Nothing was stolen. Nothing was hacked. Everything was observed — the quiet intelligence-gathering method typical of Abwehr strategy in the 1930s and early 1940s.

### Transmitting the Invisible

Late-night walks, coded letters disguised as correspondence with "relatives in Europe," and occasional trips to less monitored ports allowed them to forward their findings. Their messages were sparse, cautious, and designed to avoid any patterns that counterintelligence could trace.

### Psychological Fractures: The Cost of Living Two Truths

The paradise around them could not erase the emotional corrosion of deceit. Maintaining a double life meant living in a constant psychological split — loyalty versus survival, duty to homeland versus attachment to adopted home.

### Fear as a Constant Companion
They woke with the knowledge that one slip — one careless comment, one mistimed glance, one coded message misread — could lead to arrest, exposure, or execution. Daily life became a delicate balancing act, where every interaction contained a hidden risk.

### Conflicts of the Heart
Despite ideological ties to Germany or pressures from the Abwehr, fragments of genuine affection for America crept into their lives.
They developed bonds with neighbors, shared milestones with friends, watched their children flourish in island culture.
Paradise softened convictions — but it also deepened guilt.

Some family members felt pride in helping the Fatherland. Others questioned the moral gravity of betraying a country that had offered them safety and opportunity. These internal divisions created silent wars within the household.

### Children Growing Up Between Worlds

For the younger members, the double life was even more disorienting. They were raised singing American songs in school yet warned at home to guard their words. They learned to hide photographs, avoid certain questions, and obey unspoken rules about secrecy they did not fully understand.

As they matured, some became complicit, assisting with innocuous tasks that subtly supported espionage. Others grew resentful, realizing that their parents' hidden loyalties threatened the stability of the life they loved.

**Balancing on the Edge: The Tensions Before Pearl Harbor**
By 1941, global tensions amplified the strain of maintaining their outward façade. FBI surveillance increased. Military intelligence grew less trusting. The family sensed that the island's atmosphere had shifted from calm to charged anticipation. Paradise felt smaller, more suffocating. Every day required greater discipline, sharper instincts, and deeper emotional resilience.

They were still living in warm beaches and gentle breezes, but inside, they stood on a knife's edge — one misstep from exposure

# CHAPTER 2 — THE RISING TIDE: NAZI ESPIONAGE EXPANDS INTO THE PACIFIC

## *Berlin's Pacific Strategy and the Race for Intelligence*

As Europe spiraled into total war in the late 1930s, the German high command understood a critical geopolitical truth: the coming conflict would not be won in Europe alone. It would stretch across oceans, continents, and colonial territories where empires collided and alliances shifted with each passing month. For Berlin, the Pacific — vast, resource-rich, and strategically dominated by the United States and its territories — represented both a distant frontier and a crucial pressure point. If Germany could weaken American influence or obtain foreknowledge of U.S. military activities in the region, it could shape the global balance of power. Thus the Pacific became not simply a battlefield of nations, but a new theater of clandestine competition.

### A Region of Opportunity for Axis Ambitions

By the late 1930s, German strategists recognized that the Pacific was undergoing rapid militarization. Imperial Japan, Germany's soon-to-be Axis partner, was aggressively expanding its reach across East Asia, capturing territories and establishing new naval strongholds. Meanwhile, the United States consolidated its own Pacific defenses, particularly around Hawaii, Guam, and the Philippines. These islands, once mere colonial outposts, had become stepping-stones for American power projection into Asia.

To Berlin, this convergence of American and Japanese interests represented both a danger and an opening. While Germany viewed Japan as an ally against Western colonial dominance, it also understood that Japan's expansion could trigger direct conflict with the United States — a conflict that would inevitably drag American resources, attention, and manpower away from Europe. For Nazi strategists, any U.S. vulnerability was a potential advantage. Therefore, monitoring American naval movements, political sentiments, and defense preparations in the Pacific became a priority.

## Intelligence as a Global Weapon

The Abwehr — Germany's military intelligence service — expanded its overseas networks during this period, deploying agents, informants, and sympathizers into key regions where open war had not yet erupted. Unlike the Gestapo, the Abwehr specialized in subtlety: infiltration, observation, and manipulation rather than brute force. Its mission in the Pacific was not to destabilize governments but to quietly harvest information about enemy capabilities long before direct conflict determined the outcome.

**Identify shifts in U.S. military deployments.**

Battleships, carriers, destroyers — their movements acted as signals of American intent. Knowing where they were headed could help the Axis predict future confrontations.

**Evaluate American readiness for war.**

Training drills, supply chain patterns, construction projects, and communications security all revealed crucial details about whether the United States was preparing to defend or attack.

**Monitor diplomatic tensions.**

German intelligence tracked how American, British, Dutch, and Japanese negotiations fluctuated. Even minor changes in communication patterns hinted at deeper geopolitical strategies.

To achieve these goals, the Abwehr did not rely solely on trained German operatives — it cultivated networks of immigrants, expatriates, disaffected travelers, ambitious businessmen, and families whose ancestral ties connected them emotionally or culturally to the "old country." These individuals, especially those living in strategic territories, became valued assets.

**Why Hawaii Became a Focal Point**

Hawaii, more than any other Pacific location, became central to Berlin's ambitions — not because Germany planned an invasion, but because Pearl Harbor was the single most concentrated symbol of American naval might. The base's shipyards, submarine pens, fuel depots, radio stations, and reconnaissance posts created a web of military activity that offered extraordinary insight into U.S. strategy

The Abwehr understood that even small pieces of information — schedules, maintenance delays, training routines — could be invaluable to its intelligence partners. Germany and Japan did not share every secret, but they exchanged enough strategic data to influence each other's wartime assessments. Any hint of American vulnerability at Pearl Harbor was therefore not merely a curiosity but a potential tipping point in global military planning.

### Expansion Through Intermediaries

Berlin's Pacific intelligence operations expanded through indirect channels. German consulates in Asia, shipping companies, radio technicians, and sympathetic nationalist movements all provided cover for the slow but steady infiltration of Abwehr networks. Civilian maritime routes were especially useful. Commercial shipping lines carried more than goods — they conveyed coded messages, discreet passengers, and "businessmen" whose real work was mapping naval installations under the guise of trade.

In this wider strategy, Hawaii emerged as both a target and a crossroads. Ships passing through Honolulu brought gossip, observations, and rumors gathered from ports across the Pacific. Travelers who stayed with German-descended families on the islands could pass along subtle hints that, once decoded and assembled, revealed larger patterns. The race for intelligence was not a dramatic game of stolen documents but a patient accumulation of details.

### The Abwehr's Strategic Expectation

By 1940, Berlin's Pacific strategy rested on a critical expectation: the United States would eventually be forced into conflict, either directly with Germany or indirectly through Japan. To prepare, Germany needed early warning signals. Who better to provide those signals than families, immigrants, and expatriates living in the heart of America's Pacific fortress — individuals who could blend seamlessly into the tropical landscape while quietly reporting what they observed?

The expansion of Nazi espionage into the Pacific was not an overnight surge but a rising tide — steady, quiet, and unnervingly adaptive. Every new informant, every intercepted rumor, every observation of fleet movement added momentum to Berlin's overarching mission: to stay ahead in a global intelligence race where information, not armies, delivered the first decisive blows

# Honolulu's Hidden Networks and Foreign Agents

Long before the first Japanese aircraft appeared over Oahu's skyline on December 7, 1941, Honolulu was already a simmering hub of global espionage — a tropical crossroads where foreign agents, commercial spies, political radicals, and opportunistic informants blended almost invisibly into the colorful fabric of island life. With its bustling harbor, booming tourism, multicultural population, and strategic military presence, the city offered both rich opportunities and subtle cover for clandestine activity. Honolulu looked like paradise, but beneath its breezy palm trees and sunny beaches lay an undercurrent of quiet manipulation, coded messages, and shadowy relationships that foreign powers — including Germany — exploited with increasing sophistication.

## A City of Many Nations, Many Loyalties

By the 1930s, Honolulu had become a melting pot of cultures: Native Hawaiians, Americans from the mainland, Japanese immigrants and their descendants, Chinese and Filipino laborers, European expatriates, and merchants from across the Pacific. This diversity gave the city a cosmopolitan character, but it also created fertile ground for outside intelligence services. Different communities maintained ties to their countries of origin, reading foreign newspapers, attending cultural events, and corresponding with relatives overseas. For most residents, these connections were innocent extensions of heritage. For foreign agencies, however, they were potential pathways — openings into private networks where subtle influence or recruitment could begin.

The German Abwehr, Imperial Japan's intelligence agencies, and even Soviet operatives observed Honolulu's unique social structure and understood something vital: a spy did not need to look like James Bond or wear a trench coat. A spy could be a shopkeeper, a radio technician, a businessman, a bartender in Waikiki, or a recent immigrant working in the docks. Ordinary people, especially those belonging to close-knit ethnic groups, could pass invaluable information simply by being present and unnoticed in everyday spaces.

### The Harbor as a Magnet for Espionage

Honolulu Harbor was the beating economic heart of the city, drawing sailors, merchants, and shipping magnates from every direction. Its constant activity made it a prime target for espionage. Ships arriving from Japan, Germany, China, and even neutral countries carried passengers whose true identities were known only to a select few. On the docks, cargo manifests revealed what the city imported and exported — information that hinted at military construction, resource shortages, or changes in naval logistics.

**Foreign agents often disguised themselves as:**

- crew members on merchant vessels,
- engineers inspecting shipping equipment,
- businessmen negotiating trade deals,
- journalists supposedly covering Pacific commerce,

or transient travelers passing through on their way to Australia or South America.

In reality, many took the opportunity to discreetly survey the naval base at Pearl Harbor, note patrol patterns, observe supply shipments, or gather gossip from sailors relaxing in Honolulu's bars and hotels.

### Information Through Social Circles

Most espionage in Honolulu did not rely on dramatic acts of theft or infiltration. Instead, it flowed quietly through conversations. Honolulu's nightlife was a mixture of tiki bars, jazz lounges, social clubs, and beachfront cottages where servicemen mingled with civilians. It was in these spaces that foreign agents — especially those working indirectly for the Abwehr — listened carefully to talk about:

- ship repair schedules,
- submarine sightings,
- fuel shortages,
- new construction at Pearl Harbor,
- changes in command,

- or rumors of impending deployments

Young naval officers often drank freely and spoke openly, unaware that someone at the next table was memorizing every detail. Even innocent remarks became intelligence when combined with reports from other informants.

## The German Presence in Honolulu

Though smaller than the Japanese or Chinese communities, Honolulu's German expatriate population included merchants, teachers, plantation workers, musicians, and skilled professionals. Many were peaceful residents with no interest in the war unfolding in Europe. Yet, among them existed a handful of individuals with sympathies to the Fatherland or connections to German political groups dating back to the 1920s and 1930s.

The Abwehr recognized that such communities offered excellent camouflage. Agents or informants with German heritage could blend in as ordinary immigrants or naturalized Americans. Cultural gatherings, German-language clubs, and expatriate social events provided discreet opportunities to share coded information or assess who might be quietly supportive of Germany's cause.

In some cases, families with divided loyalties became conduits for intelligence — passing along observations of military activity simply because they felt an emotional bond to the homeland or resentment toward American policies. These informal networks formed the backbone of more structured espionage operations.

## Japanese Intelligence and the Shadow It Cast

Japan's intelligence network in Honolulu was far more extensive and organized than Germany's, but its presence provided indirect benefits to every foreign power, including Nazi Germany. Japanese consulates, commercial offices, and cultural associations often served as cover for information gathering. Their activities — from mapping shorelines to monitoring ship movements — created an atmosphere where clandestine activity could flourish without drawing immediate suspicion.

Where Japanese operatives worked systematically, other foreign agents learned to operate within the noise they created. In a sense, Japanese espionage acted as a canopy under which smaller, quieter networks — including German ones — could operate with reduced risk of exposure.

## The Role of Local Intermediaries

What made Honolulu's hidden networks truly effective was the participation of intermediaries — individuals not formally trained as spies but willing to pass along observations, carry letters, or relay coded messages. They were ordinary people drawn in for personal, political, or financial reasons:

- business owners seeking special favors,
- sailors disillusioned with their superiors,
- immigrants with lingering national loyalties,
- opportunists needing extra income,
- and families caught between two worlds.

These intermediaries gave foreign powers access not just to military information but to the social pulse of Honolulu — its gossip, its anxieties, its daily rhythms.

**A City at Peace, A World at War**

What made Honolulu's espionage ecosystem so effective was the contrast between the city's tranquil appearance and the storm building far across the Pacific. Locals surfed, shopped, worked, and danced while foreign agents quietly pieced together a mosaic of intelligence that would eventually be used to strike at America's most vital Pacific asset.

Honolulu was not just a paradise. It was a chessboard — and every foreign agent, from the most skilled spy to the most unsuspecting immigrant, was a potential piece in a global game whose final move was approaching faster than anyone realized

# Covert Dead Drops, Secret Codes, and Radio Silence

Espionage in Honolulu did not operate through grand missions or cinematic feats of danger. Instead, it thrived in the quiet spaces — the forgotten corners of back alleys, the anonymous pages of letters mailed across oceans, and the faint pulses of radio transmissions whispering into the night. The true strength of foreign intelligence networks in Hawaii rested not on dramatic sabotage but on the invisible infrastructure of secrecy: dead drops, coded messages, and controlled radio silence. These were the tools that bound together scattered informants, kept surveillance undetected, and allowed Berlin and Tokyo to gather information from the heart of America's Pacific defenses without revealing their reach.

**Dead Drops: The Art of Leaving Something Behind**

Dead drops were the lifeblood of covert communication on the islands. Honolulu's landscape — with its beaches, parks, dense tropical vegetation, and bustling markets — offered ample hiding places where information could be exchanged without two individuals ever meeting in person. To the untrained eye, they were meaningless objects; to a trained operative, they were the beating heart of a secret network.

**A dead drop might be:**

- A hollowed-out coconut wedged between rocks along Ala Moana Beach
- A small tin container buried beneath the roots of a hibiscus bush in a public garden
- A folded newspaper left on a bench in Thomas Square, marked by a single pencil stroke

A seashell placed on a specific step of a coastal trail

A coded note hidden in the lining of a jacket donated to a pawn shop

Each drop followed a rhythm: information placed quietly during the early morning or late evening, then retrieved hours or days later by someone who appeared to be merely strolling, shopping, or enjoying the ocean breeze. These passive exchanges allowed operatives to avoid risky face-to-face meetings and created a communication pipeline that was nearly impossible to trace.

Honolulu's multicultural environment made these drops even more effective. With tourists, sailors, and laborers constantly circulating through the city, a stranger pausing to tie a shoelace or check a map drew little attention. This anonymity was the very essence of covert communication.

## Secret Codes: The Hidden Language of Espionage

Far more important than the physical dead drops were the coded messages used to disguise intelligence within everyday correspondence. Foreign agents in Honolulu relied on sophisticated and subtle methods — not the dramatic cipher wheels often imagined, but techniques woven seamlessly into ordinary life. Letters to relatives abroad carried invisible layers of meaning: one misplaced adjective signaled urgency, a specific phrase meant danger, and the positioning of certain words conveyed ship departures, troop movements, or construction updates at Pearl Harbor.

**Common techniques included:**

- **Steganography:** hiding messages within innocent text, such as travel descriptions, recipes, or news commentary.
- **Invisible ink:** often lemon juice, milk, or chemical compounds revealed only with heat.
- **Grille ciphers:** decoding by placing a template over a newspaper or handwritten letter.
- **Keyword patterns:** where certain words corresponded to predetermined intelligence categories.

Numeric sequences embedded in addresses or return names.

Because these methods used real letters carried by normal postal routes, little suspicion arose. A letter describing the weather in Honolulu or the beauty of a beach sunset could be masking descriptions of naval ships, aircraft routes, or supply shipments. A postcard sent from Waikiki might conceal an entire intelligence report

Even Honolulu's German and Japanese-language newspapers played a role. Advertisements, social notices, or innocuous announcements occasionally contained coded references. Honolulu's immigrant communities, with their accustomed multilingual communications, provided an ideal environment for messages that could pass through American censors without attracting undue scrutiny.

**Radio Silence: The Discipline of Knowing When Not to Speak**

While some intelligence networks relied on radio transmission, Honolulu's foreign agents often practiced something more subtle — strategic radio silence. Sending messages over radio waves was risky; American counterintelligence monitored frequencies regularly, and any unusual signal could expose an entire network.

Thus, the most dangerous and skilled operatives used radios sparingly, if at all. Instead, they sent information through couriers, letters, or maritime routes. When a radio was used, it followed strict protocols:

- Short bursts under 20 seconds to minimize triangulation
- Randomized transmission times to avoid pattern detection
- Use of codebooks with rapidly shifting encryption tables
- Low-power signals to blend into atmospheric static

- Relay through intermediary stations in East Asia or Latin America

These methods allowed messages to blend into the ambient noise of global communications. A brief pulse of numbers late at night could be dismissed as interference unless one knew exactly how to listen.

Radio silence also meant knowing when to remain completely quiet. In the weeks before Pearl Harbor, as tensions escalated, many Honolulu-based informants reduced transmissions. Instead, they relied heavily on couriers leaving by ship or aircraft, trusting physical transport over the risk of detection. This quiet period became one of the most telling signals of impending action — though American intelligence failed to interpret it at the time.

### A Web Without a Face

What made Honolulu's covert communication methods so powerful was not the complexity of each technique but the way they interlocked to form a resilient, flexible system. Dead drops supported coded letters; coded letters reduced the need for radio transmissions; radio silence protected the identities of those using dead drops. Each method compensated for the weaknesses of the others.

And at the center of this intricate web were families — immigrants, workers, shopkeepers — whose participation was often hidden behind the normalcy of everyday routines. Their quiet acts of compliance or conviction helped maintain an invisible pipeline of information that stretched from the laneways of Honolulu to the shadowed offices of Berlin and Tokyo.

Espionage in Honolulu was never loud. It was a whisper carried on ocean winds, a folded scrap of paper left under a stone, a phrase hidden inside a letter home — a network defined not by its daring but by its silence

## *The Family's Role in Mapping the Naval Presence at Pearl Harbor*

In the vast and volatile landscape of World War II espionage, some of the most impactful intelligence came not from high-ranking officers or daring saboteurs, but from families living quietly on the periphery of conflict—embedded in the daily flow of life, unnoticed and underestimated. The family at the center of this story embodied this crucial role. Positioned just miles from the bustling naval hub of Pearl Harbor, they became an unassuming yet indispensable part of the Nazi intelligence apparatus, tasked with an assignment both delicate and perilous: mapping the naval presence at one of America's most vital military installations.

### An Unseen Frontline: The Strategic Importance of Pearl Harbor

Pearl Harbor was more than a harbor—it was the fulcrum of American naval power in the Pacific. The base was a sprawling complex of docks, fuel depots, airfields, communication centers, and repair yards. Its importance made it a magnet for spies and intelligence operatives from multiple nations. Mapping the movements and status of the ships anchored there was a key priority for the German Abwehr and its Japanese counterparts, as this information would offer a tactical edge in anticipating American responses to Axis moves in the Pacific.

The family's proximity to the base, through residence and employment, gave them unique access to critical observations. Their shop, located within walking distance of the harbor's perimeter, served as a quiet vantage point for noting daily naval rhythms. The information they gathered was subtle but invaluable: which ships were docked, which were undergoing repairs, changes in personnel rotations, and even shifts in supply deliveries.

Eyes and Ears on the Ground: Gathering Intelligence Through Observation

Unlike dramatic wartime espionage depictions, the family's work involved patience, routine, and vigilance. Their daily tasks blended seamlessly into ordinary life, masking their true intent.

- **Visual Surveillance:** Family members made detailed notes of ship silhouettes, hull numbers, and distinguishing features. Even slight variations in the ships' configurations—such as changes in armaments, flags, or personnel on deck—were meticulously recorded.

- **Traffic Patterns:** Observing which ships came and went, the timing of arrivals and departures, and the frequency of military transports provided clues about upcoming missions or resupply efforts.

- **Harbor Activity:** Supply deliveries, especially of fuel and munitions, were monitored closely. Delays or increased volume could signal shifts in operational tempo or preparation for offensive actions.

- **Communication Signals:** While direct interception was beyond their means, they paid attention to visible communication signals—flag hoists, semaphore signals, and radio antenna setups—that suggested shifts in naval command or alerts.

Each observation was coded and transmitted carefully, ensuring it could be understood by Abwehr analysts without exposing the family's role

**The Use of Local Knowledge: Navigating the Harbor's Complex Geography**

The family's deep knowledge of Honolulu and Pearl Harbor's geography allowed them to exploit vantage points invisible to many outsiders.

- **<u>Neighborhood Surveillance Points:</u>** From their home and shop windows, and discreet locations such as hilltops and quiet beach coves, they had line-of-sight to key sections of the harbor.
- **<u>Trusted Contacts:</u>** They established connections with dockworkers, supply clerks, and sailors who, unknowingly or otherwise, provided snippets of information through casual conversations or offhand remarks.
- **<u>Maritime Traffic:</u>** By tracking the harbor's comings and goings with an almost obsessive focus, they could identify patterns and anomalies that hinted at secretive maneuvers or operational pauses.

This local expertise allowed the family to compile a living map of naval activity—one that evolved daily and fed the larger intelligence network.

**Covert Communication: From Notes to Networks**
Reporting the gathered intelligence required as much care as its collection.

- **Coded Logs:** The family kept detailed logs written in code, using innocuous terms to represent ships, locations, and events.
- **Dead Drops and Couriers:** These notes were deposited at predetermined locations, often without direct contact between agents, to avoid detection.
- **Invisible Ink and Hidden Messages:** Some information was concealed in letters or postcards sent under the guise of family correspondence to contacts in the mainland or abroad.
- **Radio Silence and Timing:** The family coordinated transmissions to minimize exposure, often timing their actions to coincide with busy city activities or during hours when surveillance was lighter.

The intelligence they provided was carefully analyzed by Abwehr officers who understood how to piece together these fragments into a coherent picture of American naval disposition.

**The Weight of Secrecy: Psychological and Moral Dimensions**
Living a double life required the family to bear a heavy psychological burden.

- **The Constant Fear of Exposure:** Every day brought the risk of being caught by American counterintelligence or informants loyal to the U.S. government.

- **Balancing Normalcy and Espionage:** They had to maintain the appearance of ordinary citizens—running their shop, socializing with neighbors, raising children—while covertly watching and reporting on the military's most sensitive secrets.

- **Moral Ambiguity:** Some family members struggled with the implications of their actions—betraying the country that had become their home in service of a distant and controversial regime.

Yet the family's loyalty to their heritage, combined with pressure and perhaps coercion from Abwehr handlers, kept them engaged in this perilous game.

**Impact and Legacy**

Though the family's work remained hidden for decades, their role was a vital component of the broader Nazi intelligence campaign in the Pacific. The detailed mapping of Pearl Harbor's naval presence contributed to the Axis powers' understanding of American capabilities and vulnerabilities.

Their efforts underscore a crucial reality of World War II espionage: that war was not only fought with guns and bombs but with eyes and ears in unexpected places—quiet families who, beneath the sun-soaked surface of American paradise, shaped history through acts of secrecy and survival.

# CHAPTER 3 — SHADOWS ON THE Harbor: SURVEILLANCE, SECRETS, AND SILENT SIGNALS

## *Observing the Fleet: Daily Life Among the Enemy*

The harbor always looked peaceful at first glance—water glistening beneath the Hawaiian sun, gulls slicing through blue air, and the rhythmic hum of naval machinery echoing like a heartbeat. But for a family living dual identities, every ripple in the water and every whistle from a sailor could carry a coded meaning. In Pearl Harbor, serenity was an illusion. Under the surface was a world where shadows moved with purpose, and every day brought a new test of loyalty, discipline, and absolute silence. This was the world the Nakamura family inhabited—Americans by address, observers by necessity, ghosts by design.

From the outside, their life appeared ordinary. A modest wooden house near the shoreline. Children walking to school with books tucked under their arms. A mother writing in her garden as the breeze curled through the plumeria trees. A father who boarded the bus for "factory work" every morning.

Neighbors waved. Mail arrived on time. Nothing about them drew attention. And that was exactly the point. Their ordinary existence was the camouflage behind which an extraordinary responsibility was carried out: monitoring the movements, schedules, and behaviors of the U.S. Pacific Fleet and relaying those observations through subtle, silent signals.

Daily life among the enemy required discipline that bordered on art. The family's routines were crafted with the precision of a military drill. Every action had meaning. Every gesture carried weight. When the children passed through the naval housing district on their way to school, they were not simply walking—they were observing. The number of sailors unloading supply crates, the direction of patrol vehicles, the shift rotations at the shipyard gates—these details were committed to memory with the casualness of children spotting birds on telephone wires. Their innocence was their greatest shield.

At home, the mother—Emiko—conducted a different kind of surveillance. Her morning chores were synchronized with the harbor's activity. Hanging laundry outside gave her a vantage point to view the battleships moored along Battleship Row. The timing of gun-cleaning drills, the smoke rising from engine tests, the patterns of tugboats assisting larger vessels—all of it formed a puzzle she assembled day by day. To anyone watching, she was simply keeping a tidy home. To the family's hidden mission, she was an essential analyst, piecing together the daily rhythm of the U.S. Navy.

The father, Kenji, was the nucleus of their intelligence network. Working near the naval shipyard, he interacted with laborers who serviced aircraft, machinery, and storage warehouses. He never asked questions—only listened. Casual conversations, frustrated complaints, floating rumors about fuel shortages or sudden drills: these were clues. He had mastered the subtle craft of appearing disengaged while absorbing everything. His posture stayed relaxed, his tone friendly, his face unreadable. Behind the mask of a quiet worker, he mapped out patterns that outsiders would never notice—supply movements, officer visits, irregular shipments, and shifts in security presence.

But the family did not rely solely on individual observations. Their greatest method of information transfer was silence itself. Signals were embedded within ordinary home routines to communicate without speaking. Three clipped strokes of the garden rake meant Kenji had noticed increased aircraft activity. A misplaced teacup on the kitchen counter signaled that new officers had arrived at the dock. A laundry sheet hung slightly crooked indicated a battleship had returned earlier than scheduled. These domestic gestures—mundane to anyone else—were the family's coded language, their silent messaging system that wove their observations into a coherent picture.

Every evening, after dinner, the family reenacted the day's events in memory alone. They never discussed surveillance openly. Instead, each person contributed through routine actions. The children sorted their schoolbooks in specific patterns. Emiko arranged the dinner bowls in sequences that represented ship names or movements. Kenji used the way he folded his shirt sleeves to classify urgency. This ritual allowed them to compile intelligence without a single spoken word, ensuring that even thin walls, open windows, or roaming neighbors would never betray them.

Living among the enemy required emotional mastery as well. Fear had no place in their home. They learned to smile while standing in the shadow of warships that could destroy entire coasts. They learned to laugh when soldiers joked nearby, even though those same men would be casualties if conflict erupted. The children became experts at pretending to be carefree, even as they memorized aircraft tail numbers and officer badges. Emiko learned to calm her heartbeat when patrol boats cruised past their shoreline. Kenji learned to sleep lightly, listening for unusual footsteps or knocks in the night. Their allegiance to secrecy demanded that they not only observe the fleet but also blend seamlessly into its world.

Pearl Harbor itself was a stage of contradictions. Sailors played baseball near the water while battleships loomed behind them. Families picnicked under palm trees while gun mounts sat ready only a few yards away. The hum of daily life mixed with the underlying tension of geopolitical turmoil. The Nakamuras lived at the intersection of these two realities—immersed in American routines while serving a mission that relied on remaining invisible within those routines.

The fleet's daily movements became almost musical to them. Morning bugles signaled wake-up drills. Afternoon engine roars marked aircraft tests. The deep bellow of ship horns at dusk marked departures or returns. The family learned these sounds like notes in a symphony, identifying which vessel was active, which crew was preparing for deployment, and which sectors of the harbor were shifting in priority. The harbor spoke constantly—through smoke, sound, motion, and energy—and the Nakamuras listened with unwavering attention

Yet the most challenging part of their mission was the subtlety required to avoid suspicion. Observing the fleet was not about dramatic espionage or secret infiltrations. It was about patience—the slow, methodical accumulation of details. The family understood that even a single misstep, a single glance held too long at a battleship, or a single misplaced word in a casual conversation could unravel years of carefully constructed anonymity. Their survival depended on being forgettable.

And so they lived in the shadows of Pearl Harbor—ordinary on the surface, extraordinary beneath. They blended into the hum of daily life while quietly monitoring the largest naval presence in the Pacific. In the stillness of the harbor and the chaos of the shipyard, they found clarity. Their silent signals, domestic codes, and unspoken unity bound them together as a single, unbreakable unit. Observing the fleet required courage; living among the enemy required genius. The Nakamura family possessed both.

In this fragile world where suspicion lurked behind every uniform and whispers could shift destinies, the family of spies continued their daily vigil—watching, listening, understanding. And through their eyes, the shadows on the harbor deepened, preparing for the storm that history would one day remember

## *Smuggling Photographs and Naval Movements to Axis Hands*

The work of gathering intelligence was only half of the Nakamura family's mission; the other half—far more dangerous, far more delicate—was transmitting it without revealing their true allegiance. Observation required discipline, but smuggling required brilliance. The quiet notes, coded gestures, and silent signals were only useful if they reached the hands they were intended for. The Axis powers relied on shadows, not noise, and shadows were the Nakamuras' specialty. Every photograph, every detail of naval movement, every shift in patrol structure had to be slipped out of Pearl Harbor like a single drop of ink dissolving into the Pacific.

The family never openly discussed how they moved information. Words were risks. Silence was survival. Their entire system of smuggling evolved slowly over years, shaped by caution, necessity, and the unpredictable rhythms of life around the naval base. The U.S. fleet towered before them—battleships anchored like steel mountains, aircraft glinting in the sun, destroyers slicing through the harbor—and it was their responsibility to ensure that every observable movement, no matter how small, reached watchers far beyond the Hawaiian horizon.

Photography was the most dangerous element of their work. Taking pictures of military installations was explicitly forbidden, and the naval police patrolled the harbor with increasing vigilance. Cameras drew suspicion, and anyone caught photographing warships faced immediate arrest. But Emiko had perfected a technique that turned photography into an art of invisibility. Hidden in her kitchen cabinet, nestled behind flour tins and tea boxes, was a compact camera with a noise-dampening cloth, small enough to fit in her sleeve and powerful enough to capture distant details with startling clarity.

She never aimed directly at the ships; that would have been too obvious. Instead, she photographed through layers—slats in a drying rack, the edges of hanging laundry, gaps between potted plants. Her shots were angled like casual household pictures, the kind neighbors might take to show a blooming garden or a scenic view. Only upon closer inspection would the details within the frame reveal the silhouettes of battleships, the number of aircraft on deck, or subtle modifications to weapon mounts.

Kenji handled the most crucial—and riskiest—photographic opportunities. Working near the shipyard meant he saw what others missed. Crates of ammunition, new aircraft parts, secretive deliveries that arrived at dawn, officers holding hurried meetings in restricted areas—Kenji captured these moments in slivers. His camera was disguised as a tool, its shutter masked by the clatter of machinery. Each photograph he took carried a weight heavier than metal; it held the pulse of the Pacific Fleet.

Once the film was captured, the second challenge emerged: how to move it out of their home without being detected. The family developed an ingenious system of concealment. The children played a vital role, their backpacks and pencil cases serving as unsuspected transport. No one questioned a child carrying books or snacks. Inside false-bottom compartments, thin strips of film—rolled tightly and wrapped in waxed paper—traveled safely to the Nakamuras' network contacts.

One of these contacts was Mr. Tanabe, a local shopkeeper whose general store served as a meeting point for dozens of families. To the American community, he was a friendly merchant with a warm smile and a reputation for selling the freshest vegetables. To the Nakamuras, he was a gatekeeper. The family never handed him anything directly; instead, the children purchased sweets wrapped in small, wax-coated papers. Hidden beneath one wrapper in every batch was a strip of film or a coded message inked with a solution that appeared invisible unless heated.

Another contact operated through the fishermen who worked the shoreline. These men had no idea that their regular hauls of mackerel and tuna served double purposes. Kenji would visit the docks under the pretense of buying the day's catch. The fisherman would sell him a fish with a slightly thicker belly— inside which rested a waterproof capsule. Within that capsule, messages or photographs could travel down the coast to a boat that carried Axis sympathizers aboard. The sea became a courier, its tides washing intelligence far from Pearl Harbor before anyone could question it.

But smuggling wasn't always physical. Much of it relied on coded signals embedded in everyday life. Strings of laundry formed patterns viewed from afar by operatives with binoculars. A blue kimono hung next to a white sheet signaled a battleship's departure. A kimono patterned with waves indicated increased aerial activity. A kimono with floral prints meant officers had arrived for inspection.

When photographs or film had to travel farther—off the island entirely—the process became even more intricate. A traveling salesman, a musician touring inter-island venues, and even a mail courier who unknowingly carried hollowed-out parcel tubes became channels for intelligence. Every individual in the network had a role, even if most never knew the true nature of what they transported.

Yet the most astonishing method the family used was hidden in plain sight: radio static. Each night, after the house fell quiet and the children pretended to sleep, Kenji adjusted a small transmitter disguised as a broken shortwave radio. Buried beneath layers of static and disguised as amateur signals, he tapped out coded information—distorted enough to avoid easy detection, precise enough for trained ears thousands of miles away to understand. Naval movements, fuel shortages, departures, repairs—each detail drifted across the Pacific under the cloak of radio noise

For every successful transmission, the danger multiplied. Patrols grew more watchful. Military police questioned more residents. The harbor buzzed with whispers of possible spies. But the Nakamuras pressed on. They operated like shadows— steady, quiet, untraceable. They knew that any mistake could end not only their mission but their lives. And yet, the work continued because stopping was never an option. The fate of nations depended on the whisper-thin margin between silence and discovery.

The smuggling of photographs and naval movements was not an act of arrogance or thrill. It was an act of calculation—a chess game played on a board of steel warships and silent waters. Every piece moved carefully. Every risk weighed. And every night, as the lights of Pearl Harbor shimmered across the Pacific, the family of spies prepared again to send the harbor's secrets into the waiting hands of a distant power

## *Japanese–German Collusion: The Sharing of Stolen Secrets*

Collaboration between nations is rarely simple in times of peace, and in times of war, it becomes a web of quiet exchanges, invisible handshakes, and coded trust. For Japan and Germany—two Axis powers bound more by their strategic aims than cultural similarity—the sharing of intelligence required a clandestine network as complex as the Pacific waters separating their ambitions. In this intricate world of covert agreements and silent operations, the Nakamura family became a single, vital thread connecting two distant war machines.

To the outside world, Germany's reach into the Pacific appeared limited. Oceans, Allied patrols, and distance created the illusion that German influence ended at the borders of Europe and North Africa. But beneath that illusion ran a hidden river of shared intelligence. Through diplomats, naval attachés, business fronts, and covert operatives, Germany and Japan maintained a dark partnership that thrived on stolen secrets—blueprints, ship movements, morale reports, industrial output charts, and technological insights. What one Axis partner learned, the other often needed. This made Pearl Harbor—a hub of American naval power—one of the most valuable sources of information in the entire world.

The Nakamuras worked for Japan, but they understood from the beginning that intelligence rarely stopped at national borders. Their handlers expected them to gather information useful not only to Tokyo, but also to Berlin. And so their mission extended beyond the Pacific. Every coded message, every smuggled photograph, every whispered detail about ship repairs or fuel shortages, traveled along a shared pipeline that fed two nations with a single appetite: weakening the Allied powers.

Japanese–German collusion was not an overnight arrangement. It was built through years of diplomatic exchanges, secret military meetings, and mutual distrust of the West. German officers visiting Tokyo often brought gifts—advanced radio equipment, encryption devices, mechanical designs—while Japanese officers shared insights from their rapid modernization of naval warfare. The relationship was not always equal, nor entirely comfortable, but both sides recognized the necessity. Japan had proximity to American bases; Germany had decades of espionage expertise and a web of agents stretching across continents. Together, they formed an intelligence partnership capable of reshaping global strategy.

In Honolulu, the collusion took on a far more intimate form. Hidden within the Japanese consulate—before its closure and evacuation—were encrypted channels specifically designated for German communication. These channels, monitored quietly and discreetly, allowed reports from Pearl Harbor to travel through Tokyo and then reroute to Berlin. But diplomats were not the only couriers. German businessmen operating under neutral or innocent guises used cargo routes between Asia and Europe to transport sealed pouches filled with intelligence materials. Books, toys, and even paintings served as clever containers for microfilm hidden under layers of varnish or sewn into bindings.

One such courier, known to the Nakamuras only as "Herr Vogel," operated a shipping company with offices in Yokohama and Hamburg. He visited Hawai'i under the cover of trade negotiations years before hostilities escalated, becoming familiar with the island's geography and social patterns. Although he left before tensions erupted, the network he helped to build remained active. Even after his departure, ships connected to his company transported intelligence materials disguised as business documents or commodity lists. Every month or two, a crate of machine parts bound for Shanghai or Manila carried a smaller, concealed crate within it—packed with Axis-bound secrets.

For the Nakamuras, the collusion meant increased pressure. Their intelligence did not end at Tokyo; it ignited strategic calculations in Berlin and beyond. A single photograph of battleships lined along Battleship Row might influence Japanese planning in the Pacific and German ambitions in the Atlantic. The family understood the gravity. One misinterpreted signal, one blurred image, one incomplete report could echo across two nations' war efforts. Consequently, the family's nightly surveillance rituals grew even more precise. Every detail mattered: the tilt of a periscope, the color of signal flags on deck, the number of sailors deployed during drills, the pace of aircraft reshuffling.

Tokyo's agents carefully selected the information that Germany would receive. Some of it was routed directly to Berlin through encrypted radio frequencies that bounced across the globe, masked behind false meteorological broadcasts. Other data traveled physically—carried by diplomatic couriers or informants embedded in cargo operations. Germany valued especially the insights into U.S. industrial patterns and naval construction timelines. Japan, in return, expected support in interpreting European intelligence, understanding Allied convoy patterns, and deciphering advanced German encryption methods.

The most dangerous exchange—one that the Nakamuras were only partially aware of—concerned submarine warfare. German U-boats operated relentlessly in the Atlantic, hunting Allied supply lines. Japan sought to learn from their strategies, while Germany wanted insights into the Pacific fleet's defensive weaknesses. The photographs that the Nakamuras smuggled, depicting harbor depth, patrol schedules, or maintenance periods, became pieces of a larger mosaic. This mosaic informed German U-boat coordination thousands of miles away, allowing them to predict how American reinforcements might move between oceans.

The collusion extended beyond documents and photographs. Technology was exchanged in ways that had long-term implications. Japan received designs for improved optical equipment and radio encryption systems inspired by German engineering. In return, they provided Berlin with information about U.S. aircraft capabilities and Pacific radar experiments—information partially gathered by civilian observers like the

Nakamuras, who pieced together patterns the same way one might study the stars in the night sky

The family understood that their intelligence served more than one master, but they rarely dwelled on the politics. Their loyalty lay strictly with their Japanese handlers, yet they accepted that their reports rippled across a wider sphere. When Kenji sent coded transmissions late at night, the signals traveled much farther than he could imagine—picked up by distant listening stations, decoded by analysts in underground bunkers, and ultimately used to coordinate movements on battlefields he would never see. Emiko, as she developed photographs in the darkened pantry, sometimes paused as the images emerged—warships rising ghost-like from the paper. She wondered which nation would make use of the captured moment. Germany? Japan? Both?

For the children, German involvement was even more obscured. They only knew that their "invisible friends across the sea"—as their father once cryptically described them—valued accuracy above all. The children internalized this pressure, ensuring every observation was memorized carefully, every detail delivered flawlessly. They learned early that information was currency, traded between nations like gold.

Japanese–German collusion thrived because it was built on unspoken understanding: two different powers united by shared goals and mutual threats. Their intelligence relationship was a chain—long, fragile, and powerful. And families like the Nakamuras were its hidden links, binding distant continents together through stolen secrets, whispered codes, and shadows cast over Pearl Harbor

## *The Tightening Noose: American Counterintelligence Begins to Notice*

Even the quietest shadows eventually draw attention. For the Nakamura family, years of meticulous observation, silent signaling, and covert transmissions had passed without incident. They had become ghosts in their own neighborhood, moving unnoticed while feeding critical intelligence to their handlers. But in late 1940 and early 1941, subtle changes in Pearl Harbor's atmosphere began to signal a new danger: American counterintelligence was waking up, and the noose around spies was beginning to tighten.

At first, it was almost imperceptible. Navy security officers seemed slightly more alert during dock inspections. Guards on patrol began shifting patterns unpredictably. Questions from supervisors that once focused only on schedules or efficiency now occasionally veered toward personal routines. Were any workers taking note of unusual patterns among their neighbors? Were family activities drawing unnecessary attention? To anyone else, these shifts might have seemed mundane or bureaucratic. To the Nakamuras, they were harbingers of scrutiny.

Kenji noticed the first true signs of interest when routine shipments began to be monitored more closely. Crates that previously passed with cursory checks were now opened, inspected, and sometimes sealed with new tags. The pace of inventory logging increased, and security personnel lingered longer than necessary, glancing up at workers and pedestrians with a subtle, measured suspicion. A minor mistake—hesitation while observing a crane, an extra moment spent watching a tugboat—could be enough to spark questions. Each day, the environment became more unpredictable, more dangerous, and more suffused with tension.

The children sensed the changes too, though they could not fully articulate them. Their morning walks past the naval housing districts had always been predictable and calm. Now, unfamiliar faces began appearing along their routes. Plainclothes officers strolled through the streets, observing dockworkers, scribbling notes, or casually leaning against posts while keeping the harbor in view. The children learned to keep their heads down, to avoid drawing attention with lingering glances or whispered comments. Even small behaviors—stopping to watch a ship's engines start or to count aircraft—had to be masked in casual play, lest curiosity be mistaken for espionage.

Emiko felt the tightening noose most acutely in the home itself. Everyday routines that once allowed for coded communication—laundry patterns, table arrangements, garden signals—had to be reconsidered. Suddenly, a neighbor's visit, an unexpected mail delivery, or even the routine approach of a postal carrier could compromise a subtle message. She learned to weave codes into more obscure gestures: the precise folding of napkins, the orientation of teacups, the sequence of spice jars along the kitchen counter. Every signal had to appear natural, yet remain comprehensible to her family.

Perhaps the most alarming development came in the form of intelligence sweeps by the Office of Naval Intelligence (ONI). ONI had begun paying closer attention to the civilian populations surrounding naval facilities, particularly Japanese-American families. While no direct accusation had been leveled at the Nakamuras, the family was acutely aware that surveillance could be happening anywhere: on the street, in the market, or even across the harbor from nearby vantage points. They learned to anticipate the movements of these unseen observers, watching not just the fleet, but the watchers themselves.

Communication with Axis handlers also grew riskier. Coded transmissions—once a relatively safe practice—became potentially traceable. Radio frequencies were monitored more rigorously. Intercepts and triangulations, though still imprecise in early 1941, introduced new challenges. Kenji had to adjust transmission schedules, vary locations, and refine encoding techniques. Even the simplest lapse—a predictable schedule or a repeated pattern—could draw scrutiny. Each transmission now carried the double burden of precision and secrecy, amplifying the tension within the household.

Inside the family, discipline became a daily necessity. Mistakes were no longer abstract threats—they were potentially fatal. The children learned to compartmentalize what they observed, recording details mentally without leaving written evidence. Kenji and Emiko rehearsed signals, tested new hiding spots for microfilm, and evaluated every photograph to ensure it contained no markers that could identify them if intercepted. The stakes had escalated: the family's survival, as well as the integrity of their intelligence network, depended on vigilance, creativity, and absolute composure

Even social interactions became tests of control. Casual conversations with neighbors or friends required careful thought. Innocuous questions about a sailor's absence or a delivery schedule could inadvertently signal knowledge too precise for an ordinary civilian. Humor, once a refuge for the children, had to be tempered. Curiosity was no longer a virtue—it was a liability. Every gesture, every word, every pause could be observed, analyzed, and misinterpreted. The Nakamuras became experts in emotional regulation, mastering the art of appearing ordinary while carrying extraordinary burdens.

The tightening noose was not just operational—it was psychological. Fear crept into small spaces: the backyard where the children played, the kitchen where Emiko coded signals into ordinary movements, the living room where Kenji reviewed photographs. It manifested in quickened heartbeats when an unfamiliar car passed, in long silences after a knock at the door, and in the heightened awareness of sound, shadow, and movement. Pearl Harbor itself seemed to shift under their perception, no longer a landscape of routine but a terrain of constant, invisible threat.

Yet, even as American counterintelligence began to notice, the Nakamuras adapted. Every risk inspired a new layer of strategy: shifting observation points, rotating transmission schedules, and refining the subtlety of household codes. Their discipline, honed over years, became armor against scrutiny. They understood that the noose might tighten further, but survival demanded calm, precision, and resilience. Observing the fleet had always required courage; now, evading suspicion required ingenuity.

And so, under the bright Hawaiian sun and the ever-watchful eyes of the U.S. Navy, the family persisted. Shadows deepened, watchers multiplied, and tension rose—but the Nakamuras remained ghosts, moving in silence, feeding intelligence, and surviving in a world where one mistake could unravel years of careful work. The tightening noose was real, but it only sharpened their resolve, proving that in espionage, awareness, adaptability, and courage were the only safeguards against discovery

# CHAPTER 4 — DECEMBER APPROACHES: THE FINAL INTELLIGENCE PUSH

## *The Last Transmission: Critical Data Sent Abroad*

As November faded and December approached, the atmosphere around Pearl Harbor shifted subtly but unmistakably. The harbor, normally a rhythm of drills, maintenance, and naval ceremonies, began to pulse with increased activity. Battleships were repositioned, aircraft carriers underwent final pre-deployment checks, and crews trained with heightened intensity. To the Nakamura family, these were not just routine movements—they were signals of a looming operation, a crescendo of activity that demanded careful attention. Years of surveillance had taught them that the closer to conflict, the more valuable every detail became.

In the Nakamura household, urgency replaced routine. Emiko's observations became meticulous to the point of obsession. Every time a crane moved ammunition, every time a tugboat repositioned a destroyer, every time a group of sailors conducted drills, she noted it mentally, embedding the information into a system of silent signals. Kenji reviewed ship arrangements in the harbor from vantage points that had been memorized over years. The family's children, previously casual observers, now acted as stealthy scouts, noting the comings and goings of officers, the frequency of security patrols, and the subtle shifts in schedules that might indicate an impending military operation.

**Covert Photography and Data Collection**

The final intelligence push demanded precision in photography. Cameras were carefully concealed, and angles were meticulously chosen to capture critical information without raising suspicion. Emiko and Kenji employed a dual approach: Emiko focused on capturing overall fleet formations, identifying which battleships and cruisers were moored where and noting any modifications, while Kenji concentrated on detailed documentation of aircraft activity, armament, and logistical supplies. Each photograph was studied immediately in the pantry darkroom, ensuring that nothing was missed and that each frame was properly labeled with time, location, and observed patterns.

Microfilm became the family's lifeline to Axis handlers. High-resolution images of ships, aircraft, and strategic installations were transferred onto film strips that could be easily concealed and transported. Even a slight smudge or tear could render intelligence useless, so every frame underwent rigorous inspection. The family's nightly routines evolved into rehearsals for precision and speed, balancing observation with concealment to ensure that no detail, however minute, was overlooked.

With the stakes higher than ever, the Nakamuras relied heavily on their established system of silent communication. Ordinary household activities—folding laundry, arranging dinnerware, or positioning garden tools—became encoded messages. The sequence of kimono patterns, the tilt of teacups, or the placement of books on the shelf indicated movements of specific ships, unusual officer activity, or shifts in patrol schedules. These subtle gestures allowed information to be documented and shared internally without creating any evidence of espionage in writing or conversation.

In parallel, Kenji fine-tuned the family's radio transmissions. Encrypted signals were sent at irregular intervals to prevent triangulation. Frequencies were rotated, messages masked within layers of static, and every transmission carefully logged mentally. Even minor environmental disruptions, such as a passing storm or increased local radio interference, were accounted for to ensure that each message reached its intended destination—Axis handlers abroad—with minimal risk of interception.

### Final Verification: Cross-Checking Observations

December demanded not only the collection of information but the verification of every detail. The family cross-checked observations, comparing notes against earlier recordings and known schedules to confirm accuracy. If a battleship had shifted a few meters from its usual berth or if aircraft numbers differed from prior counts, those deviations were highlighted and emphasized in transmissions. Every deviation, no matter how minor, was potentially significant, providing clues about imminent strategic moves

Children played an unexpectedly crucial role in verification. Their ability to observe without suspicion allowed them to monitor daily shifts unnoticed by security. A child's simple note about a ship's position at a particular hour could confirm or correct an adult observation, ensuring that the final intelligence package was as precise and reliable as possible.

## The Last Transmission: Delivering Critical Intelligence

The pinnacle of the family's efforts came in the form of the last pre-attack transmission. This operation required extreme caution. A single misstep could expose the family or compromise the mission. Kenji selected a secure location outside the home, shielded from casual observation, to send a final encoded radio transmission. Each detail—ship positions, aircraft readiness, patrol patterns, and supply movements—was condensed into a concise, precise code.

Simultaneously, microfilm containing photographs of the fleet and harbor installations was packaged and sent through trusted couriers. A child's innocuous shopping trip became the vehicle for a hidden capsule; a parcel meant for a business transaction carried concealed intelligence destined for Axis contacts. The combination of physical and electronic transmission ensured redundancy, maximizing the likelihood that critical information reached Axis hands intact.

The final intelligence push was not only technical—it was profoundly psychological. Each family member carried the knowledge that the information they were transmitting could shape military operations thousands of miles away. Fear, tension, and awareness of scrutiny were constant companions. The tightening security at Pearl Harbor, the increased vigilance of U.S. intelligence officers, and the ever-present risk of exposure amplified the family's stress. Yet, it also honed their focus. Every gesture, every photograph, every transmission was executed with calm precision, a testament to years of training and discipline.

As December drew closer, the Nakamuras functioned as a single, cohesive unit. Observation, documentation, verification, encoding, and transmission became a seamless process. They had become invisible guardians of information, their eyes and hands bridging continents, delivering intelligence that would echo across the Pacific. In those final days, every movement, every detail, every silent signal mattered more than ever. Pearl Harbor itself seemed to hold its breath, and in the shadows, a family of spies prepared for the moment when their efforts would intersect with history

# Missed Warnings, Fragmented Clues, and Bureaucratic Blindness

In the weeks leading up to December, the Nakamura family observed subtle, almost imperceptible signs that something significant was imminent. Ships were moving in unusual patterns, aircraft rotations increased, and patrol schedules shifted unpredictably. Every minor anomaly—slight deviations in fuel supply chains, the appearance of unusual cargo, and changes in officer routines—was noted meticulously. To the untrained eye, these were routine adjustments in a busy naval base. To a family trained in intelligence gathering, they were signals of heightened operational activity.

Despite the Nakamuras' careful documentation, much of this intelligence never reached the right hands in a usable form. The U.S. military bureaucracy was vast, compartmentalized, and often slow to connect isolated data points. Reports of suspicious Japanese communications, increased espionage activity, and minor security anomalies were scattered across multiple offices. Analysts who might have pieced these fragmented clues together were overwhelmed by routine administrative demands, leading to missed opportunities to act on warnings.

### Fragmented Clues Across the Harbor

The family's observations were precise, accurate, and urgent, yet they were part of a larger puzzle that remained incomplete to American counterintelligence. Occasionally, sailors noted unusual behavior from local residents, naval officers commented on minor irregularities, and some routine inspections turned up unexplained documentation. These incidents, taken individually, appeared insignificant. It was only in hindsight that the mosaic of fragmented clues formed a coherent pattern—one that foreshadowed the impending attack.

For the Nakamuras, frustration mingled with fear. They were acutely aware that while their intelligence was detailed and meticulously transmitted, the recipients were often hampered by institutional inertia. Signals that could have prompted increased alertness, adjustments to defensive readiness, or further investigation were diluted within layers of bureaucratic procedure. Every piece of data—the timing of ship maintenance, the schedules of carrier exercises, the location of patrol craft—was a potential warning. Yet, in the American chain of command, these warnings were filtered, delayed, and sometimes dismissed as inconsequential.

**Communication Gaps and Misinterpretations**
Part of the failure to act on critical intelligence stemmed from how it was communicated. Reports arriving from different sources—intercepted radio signals, cryptographic decryptions, eyewitness accounts—were often incomplete or lacked corroborating details. Analysts, faced with these fragmentary messages, struggled to prioritize them. Some warnings about

potential Japanese aggression were vague or coded, and without context, they appeared speculative rather than actionable.

The Nakamuras understood this dynamic and had adapted their own reporting methods accordingly. They combined photographs, silent coded gestures, and encrypted radio transmissions to convey maximum clarity. Yet even the most precise intelligence could be misread by those not intimately familiar with the context. A note about increased ship activity at Pearl Harbor could be interpreted as a routine readiness exercise rather than a prelude to attack.

**Bureaucratic Blindness: The Cost of Routine**
Beyond communication gaps, the rigidity of military hierarchy contributed to systemic blindness. Decisions flowed through multiple levels of approval, and lower-level warnings often lost urgency as they ascended the chain of command. Officers familiar with procedural norms hesitated to escalate anomalies without explicit evidence of imminent danger. Even when cryptographic analysts decoded Japanese messages indicating unusual operational orders, the significance was often underappreciated in the context of day-to-day administrative demands.

This bureaucratic inertia created a dangerous lag between observed activity and defensive action. For the Nakamuras, who witnessed the meticulous preparation of the fleet for the coming days, this lag was alarming. They realized that despite their best efforts in surveillance and intelligence transmission, human structures of administration could inadvertently nullify the value of timely information.

**Psychological Toll on the Family**

The awareness of missed warnings imposed a heavy psychological burden on the Nakamuras. They were keenly aware that their observations, if properly interpreted and acted upon, could have altered the course of impending events. This knowledge was both a source of pride and of anxiety. Every piece of data they collected, every coded signal sent, was a silent testament to their skill—but also a reminder of how vulnerable the situation remained.

Emiko, while developing photographs in the darkened pantry, sometimes paused, realizing that the images in her hands represented truths that might never be fully recognized. Kenji, during his evening surveillance, became increasingly vigilant, knowing that even minor mistakes could result in lost opportunities. The children, though shielded from the full scope of danger, absorbed the tension and learned that espionage carried not only risk of exposure but also the burden of knowing critical truths that others might overlook.

**The Larger Picture: Inaction Amidst Abundant Clues**

The fragmented warnings, unconnected reports, and bureaucratic blind spots highlighted a systemic vulnerability.

Pearl Harbor's defenses were formidable in many respects, yet they were only as effective as the decision-making processes that guided them. In the Nakamuras' view, the combination of detailed observation and administrative lag created a perilous environment—one in which careful intelligence could arrive too late, be misinterpreted, or be disregarded altogether.

Even as December approached, the family continued their work, meticulously collecting and transmitting intelligence. They were aware that their final push would carry the most critical information yet, but they also understood that the value of their labor depended as much on human interpretation as on the accuracy of their observations. The tension between observation and action, between knowledge and bureaucratic reality, became an ever-present shadow over their daily lives.

## *Inside the Family's Mind: Fear, Ideology, and Irreversible Choices*

For the Nakamura family, espionage was not merely a profession; it was a constant psychological crucible. Every day brought the unrelenting pressure of secrecy, the ever-present threat of exposure, and the delicate balance between ordinary life and clandestine work. Fear permeated the household like a silent, invisible fog. A stray glance from a neighbor, the sudden approach of a patrol car, or even a misdirected question from a shopkeeper could trigger a cascade of anxiety. The stakes were no longer abstract; discovery meant imprisonment, interrogation, or worse, and the family understood the fragility of their position.

Fear, however, was both a burden and a tool. It sharpened their senses, demanding absolute vigilance in observation, recording, and transmission. The children learned early to mask their curiosity with innocence. Emiko and Kenji internalized protocols so deeply that routine actions—folding laundry, preparing meals, or walking through the neighborhood— became second nature, executed with the precision of a trained operative. Fear was transformed into discipline, shaping every moment of their lives with exacting rigor.

## Ideology and Conviction: The Motivating Force

While fear guided behavior, ideology fueled commitment. The Nakamuras were acutely aware of Japan's strategic ambitions and viewed their work as a form of patriotic service. Kenji often reflected on the broader narrative of national defense, understanding that their intelligence could influence the balance of power in the Pacific. Emiko internalized this sense of duty, instilling in the children a coded understanding that their observations were not just household exercises but contributions to a larger cause.

Ideology, however, was complex. It coexisted with awareness of the human cost of war. The family knew that their transmissions, photographs, and coded messages would shape military actions with potentially catastrophic consequences. Balancing this sense of duty with the ethical implications of their work created an internal tension that few outside their household could comprehend. Each act of intelligence gathering was both service and moral gamble—a calculated choice that weighed national loyalty against the potential for destruction.

### Irreversible Choices: Crossing the Point of No Return

As December approached, the family confronted the reality that their decisions were irreversible. Once a photograph was taken, a signal transmitted, or a microfilm capsule dispatched, the act could not be undone. Every decision carried consequences beyond their control. A single miscalculation could expose them to American counterintelligence or compromise operational security. The weight of these irreversible choices pressed on Kenji and Emiko daily, shaping their interactions, surveillance methods, and risk assessment.

The children, though young, sensed the gravity of these choices. Games and routines became opportunities to rehearse observation skills without raising suspicion, a subtle education in responsibility under extreme conditions. Even minor deviations—looking too long at a battleship or asking an unusual question—were internalized as potential threats. In this household, the concept of "irreversible" was not theoretical; it was tangible, ever-present, and shaping the family's behavior in real time.

### Psychological Strategies: Maintaining Composure

To navigate the tension of fear and ideology, the Nakamuras developed psychological strategies. Emiko meditated silently while developing photographs, using focus and calm to manage the pressure of their work. Kenji compartmentalized tasks, approaching each step of observation and transmission as a discrete unit rather than a portion of an overarching, perilous operation. The children were trained in situational awareness, learning to observe without emotional attachment, internalizing information methodically, and understanding that mistakes could carry catastrophic consequences.

These strategies created a delicate equilibrium. Emotion was controlled, but not eliminated; discipline countered panic, but not anxiety. The household functioned as a cohesive unit where mental resilience was as crucial as technical skill. Every family member contributed to the maintenance of this balance, knowing that the psychological state of one could compromise the mission of all

**Moral Reflection and Cognitive Dissonance**

Despite the rigor, moments of moral reflection occasionally surfaced. Emiko sometimes paused over photographs of armed battleships, realizing the information could lead to human casualties. Kenji, while sending coded radio transmissions, felt the ethical weight of the intelligence flowing into Axis hands. These reflections were not indulgent—they were a necessary reality check, a cognitive anchor that prevented them from becoming robotic in their duty.

Yet the family reconciled these tensions through ideology. By framing their actions as service to national objectives and by focusing on precision and responsibility, they managed the cognitive dissonance inherent in espionage. Duty mitigated guilt; discipline tempered moral uncertainty. This mental framework allowed them to continue operating under extreme pressure, navigating the moral and psychological landscape of their work.

**Anticipation and Anxiety: The Final Countdown**

In the final days before December 7, the family's psychological state intensified. Every observation carried heightened urgency, every signal was critical, and the margin for error had narrowed to almost zero. Sleep was lighter, gestures more deliberate, and every household activity infused with double meaning. Fear and ideology interwove tightly, creating a heightened state of awareness that was both exhausting and essential.

The Nakamuras existed in a world where thought, observation, and action were inseparable. Each family member bore the weight of irreversible choices, each informed by ideological conviction, sharpened by fear, and measured against the constant risk of exposure. The mental landscape of espionage was relentless—silent, invisible, and as consequential as any naval maneuver. In the shadows of Pearl Harbor, their minds were battlegrounds, shaping decisions that could alter the course of history

# Countdown to Disaster: The Hours Before the Attack

The psychological weight of the final hours was immense. Each family member felt the tension, the awareness that failure— even a minor lapse—could have devastating consequences. The children, trained in observation and subtle signaling, remained unusually quiet, understanding that every sound or movement could attract unwanted attention. Emiko and Kenji moved with deliberate calm, yet internally, adrenaline heightened their senses and quickened their thought processes.

The pressure of time compounded the strain. Patrol schedules, sunrise light conditions, and the precise timing of ship inspections meant that every minute was critical. Observations had to be accurate, photographs flawless, and transmissions precise. Even slight delays could render information obsolete, and any misstep could alert American security to unusual activity in the area.

**Fragmented Clues Consolidated**

In these final hours, the family worked to consolidate all previously gathered intelligence. Fragmented clues, once isolated observations, were synthesized into a coherent, actionable package. Minor anomalies noted over weeks— unexplained adjustments in anti-aircraft guns, unusual officer meetings, irregular aircraft maintenance—were now compiled and prioritized. The family understood that this was the moment when their intelligence carried the most potential impact, when every observation could alter the understanding of enemy readiness abroad.

### Anticipation of the Unknown

Even with their meticulous preparation, the Nakamuras could not predict the precise timing or method of the attack. The suspense was almost unbearable. Every sound from the harbor, every aircraft engine, every echo of footsteps could signify either routine activity or the commencement of an unprecedented strike. The family moved in synchronized caution, ensuring that their presence remained invisible, while their eyes and ears absorbed every detail with unwavering focus.

### The Final Hours: Transmission and Observation

By mid-morning, Kenji's radio transmission was complete, and the last set of microfilm capsules were dispatched through trusted channels. The photographs, sketches, and coded messages represented the culmination of months of work—the intelligence that would travel thousands of miles to Axis handlers. Each capsule, each transmission, was executed with absolute care, ensuring redundancy to safeguard against interception.

The family continued observation even after transmission, aware that the first signals of the attack could emerge at any moment. Kenji adjusted his vantage point to track the harbor's patrols, Emiko remained ready with her camera, and the children maintained silent observation posts from windows and alleys. Every second was imbued with heightened awareness, a tense vigil over the calm yet ominous waters of Pearl Harbor.

**The Calm Before Catastrophe**

As the clock inched toward late morning, an uneasy calm settled over the harbor. Ships rested in place, aircraft lay dormant but ready, and the usual bustle of sailors continued. For the Nakamuras, this calm was deceptive; it was the final pause before the inevitable storm. Years of intelligence gathering, months of coded communication, and the culmination of their final pre-attack push had all led to this precarious moment.

In these hours, the family embodied the duality of espionage: invisible observers wielding knowledge of immense consequence, and human beings navigating fear, ideology, and irreversible choices. Every sight, sound, and signal carried layered meaning. Every heartbeat echoed with anticipation, every gesture with silent urgency. In the shadows of Pearl Harbor, the Nakamuras waited, aware that history was poised on the edge of a knife, and that their work would soon intersect with the unfolding disaster

# CHAPTER 5 — INFERNO AT DAWN: PEARL HARBOR THROUGH THE EYES OF SPIES

## *The Morning of December 7, 1941*

December 7, 1941, began like any other Sunday morning in Honolulu, yet for the Nakamura family, the day carried a weight unlike any before. Dawn light spilled over the harbor, glinting off the steel hulls of battleships, cruisers, and destroyers. Sailors went about their routine drills, aircraft crews prepared planes for inspection, and the hum of diesel engines and steam turbines filled the air. To the casual observer, it was calm and orderly—a Sunday like any other. To the family of spies, however, every movement, every sound, and every signal carried a hidden meaning.

Kenji Nakamura was already at his observation point, binoculars trained on Battleship Row. Years of practice had trained his eyes to detect the slightest irregularity: the angle of a mooring line, the number of sailors on deck, or the sudden absence of an officer from a routine inspection. Each anomaly, previously recorded over months of surveillance, formed a pattern that now demanded urgent attention. He noted unusual tight formations of ships, increased aircraft alignment drills, and the presence of extra security personnel—details that signaled a heightened state of readiness and possibly the final stages of preparation for something monumental.

## Silent Observation Amid Chaos

Emiko, stationed in a concealed vantage point near the harbor edge, prepared her camera, knowing that every photograph she captured could provide crucial intelligence. She focused on aircraft positions, torpedo bomber readiness, and the alignment of carrier decks. Every frame she captured was analyzed for changes in pattern from prior days. For the Nakamuras, observation was not passive; it was active, continuous, and meticulous. Their work required both patience and instantaneous recognition of significant deviations—subtle cues that a novice observer would never perceive.

The children, trained from a young age in observation and coded signaling, quietly assisted. Their role was simple yet critical: noting minor shifts in routine, such as the timing of sentry movements, the location of small patrol craft, or the comings and goings of officers. They communicated silently through pre-arranged signals—a tilt of the head, a hand gesture, a placement of a household object—allowing information to flow within the family without raising suspicion.


## The First Signs of Catastrophe

At approximately 7:55 a.m., a distant drone of aircraft engines began to cut through the morning calm. Kenji's trained ears immediately recognized the sound as unfamiliar formations approaching at high altitude. He adjusted his focus to track the incoming aircraft, noting their flight paths and formations. Emiko, sensing the urgency, snapped rapid-sequence photographs, capturing both aircraft positions and the initial reactions of personnel on the docks. The family, though trained in years of secrecy, felt the sudden surge of adrenaline—the unmistakable realization that their intelligence had reached the point of immediate relevance.

The harbor, once a scene of orderly preparation, began to erupt into chaos. Ships' sirens sounded, alarms blared, and sailors scrambled toward defensive positions. Anti-aircraft guns were manned, yet many crews were unprepared for the speed and intensity of the attack. From her vantage point, Emiko noted torpedo bombers diving with precision, while high-altitude bombers released payloads on key targets. Smoke began to rise from damaged ships, reflecting off the morning sun and creating an inferno visible even from distant observation points.

### Documentation Amid Fire and Confusion

Even as destruction unfolded, the Nakamuras continued to document the attack. Every movement was critical: which ships were struck first, how crews responded, which areas of the harbor were most vulnerable. Kenji sketched rapid diagrams of ship positions before and after explosions, while Emiko captured photographic evidence of aircraft maneuvers and the cascading fires. The family understood that these records, though collected under extreme duress, could serve as vital intelligence for their handlers and, indirectly, inform strategic evaluations across the Pacific.

The children, silent but vigilant, continued noting smaller details—the retreat paths of sailors, the deployment of firefighting crews, and the unexpected movements of smaller patrol boats. Their observations, though seemingly minor, provided nuanced insight into the American fleet's response patterns under duress, a level of detail that would be invaluable to any analyst interpreting the attack from afar

### The Human Element: Fear, Courage, and Confusion

While observation remained the family's primary focus, the psychological impact of the attack was immediate and intense. Kenji and Emiko recognized the fear etched on sailors' faces, the confusion among officers, and the courage of those improvising defensive measures amidst chaos. Smoke, fire, and explosions created an overwhelming sensory environment, yet the Nakamuras had to maintain composure to continue their work. Every photograph, sketch, and mental note was a balancing act between survival and duty—a silent testament to their training and resolve.

The morning also revealed the limitations of prediction. Despite months of surveillance, precise timing and tactics of the attack were unknown. Yet the intelligence they had collected in prior weeks—ship positions, patrol schedules, aircraft readiness—allowed them to interpret the unfolding disaster with exceptional clarity. They could anticipate movements, understand patterns, and recognize the tactical logic behind the Japanese assault, even as the chaos overtook the harbor.

From the initial moments of attack until late morning, the Nakamuras maintained their vigil. Smoke and fire obscured vision, anti-aircraft fire created a cacophony of sound, and debris rained over the harbor. Yet every detail, every nuance of movement, was absorbed and recorded. The family understood that these observations represented a unique historical record— one created in real time, under extraordinary risk, with a level of granularity rarely available to traditional intelligence networks.

As the sun climbed higher, the scale of destruction became undeniable. Battleships were ablaze, aircraft littered the decks, and explosions continued to reshape the harbor landscape. For the Nakamuras, it was a moment of paradoxical clarity: danger was everywhere, yet their purpose—the meticulous documentation of critical intelligence—remained singular and unshaken. Every photograph, every mental note, and every coded signal represented the culmination of months of careful planning, surveillance, and disciplined observation

# *Shock, Guilt, and the Realization of Consequence*

As the smoke began to clear over Pearl Harbor, the Nakamura family emerged from their concealed observation posts, their eyes taking in the full scale of the devastation. Ships lay in ruin, fires raged across decks, and the cacophony of alarms, explosions, and frantic human activity filled the air. For years, they had trained their minds to detach from emotion during observation, but in these first moments, detachment became impossible. Shock gripped them—not for their own safety, which they had largely preserved through careful preparation—but for the sheer human cost of the assault they had witnessed in real time.

Kenji's hands shook slightly as he lowered his binoculars, realizing that the months of meticulous intelligence gathering, the coded transmissions, and the photographs now existed in stark reality. The consequences of their work, once abstract, had been crystallized in flames and twisted steel. Emiko, standing beside him, felt a deep, unspoken guilt. The knowledge she carried—the confirmation of exact ship positions, patrol schedules, and aircraft readiness—had facilitated the accuracy of the attack. The abstract duty of espionage had transformed into a tangible impact, one that inflicted death and destruction on thousands.

**The Weight of Guilt: Personal and Collective**

Guilt was immediate and pervasive. Each family member grappled with the realization that the information they had transmitted was not neutral; it had been used to lethal effect. The Nakamuras were trained in compartmentalization, but the smoke, cries, and chaos surrounding Pearl Harbor shattered that mental barrier. The images captured in Emiko's camera—the fires consuming the USS Arizona, the capsized vessels, the frantic sailors—were no longer analytical data points; they were human tragedies that could have been mitigated had their intelligence not fallen into enemy hands.

Even the children, who had been shielded from the full gravity of espionage until now, understood in instinctive ways that their work contributed to irreversible consequences. The tilt of a flag, the silent notation of a patrol schedule, and the coded gestures they had practiced for months now seemed weighty beyond comprehension. Innocence collided with the reality of war, leaving them simultaneously frightened, awed, and quietly complicit in events that exceeded their understanding.

**Recognition of Scale: The Human Cost**

As the day progressed, the Nakamuras walked cautiously through nearby streets and observation points, witnessing the scale of human suffering. Sailors scrambled to rescue shipmates, medics tended to the wounded, and civilians were caught in panic. The family's intelligence—accurate, timely, and detailed—had translated directly into the tactical advantage exploited by Japanese forces. Every destroyed aircraft, every lost ship, and every casualty underscored the profound magnitude of their actions.

Kenji and Emiko had always known espionage carried risk; what they had not fully grasped was the immediacy and scale of human cost. This realization was compounded by their intimate knowledge of what could have been avoided had warnings been connected or acted upon. They recognized that their meticulous observation, once a tool for information, had inadvertently become an instrument of destruction, an unanticipated amplifier of tragedy.

**Moral Reckoning: Ideology vs. Reality**

In the hours following the attack, ideological justifications for espionage clashed violently with the reality of devastation. The sense of national duty that had driven the family for months now seemed distant against the backdrop of smoldering battleships and wounded sailors. Kenji reflected on the paradox of service: their loyalty to an idealized cause had intersected with human suffering in ways neither could fully reconcile.

Emiko, meanwhile, processed her own moral conflict. Her ideological commitment to Japan had guided every photograph, coded message, and observation. Yet, witnessing the consequences firsthand—men trapped in flames, ships irreparably damaged, and lives lost—forced a reconsideration of previously abstract notions of duty. For the Nakamuras, ideology could no longer mask the weight of real-world impact

**Moral Reckoning: Ideology vs. Reality**

In the hours following the attack, ideological justifications for espionage clashed violently with the reality of devastation. The sense of national duty that had driven the family for months now seemed distant against the backdrop of smoldering battleships and wounded sailors. Kenji reflected on the paradox of service: their loyalty to an idealized cause had intersected with human suffering in ways neither could fully reconcile.

Emiko, meanwhile, processed her own moral conflict. Her ideological commitment to Japan had guided every photograph, coded message, and observation. Yet, witnessing the consequences firsthand—men trapped in flames, ships irreparably damaged, and lives lost—forced a reconsideration of previously abstract notions of duty. For the Nakamuras, ideology could no longer mask the weight of real-world impact.

**Psychological Trauma: Coping with Reality**

The immediate emotional aftermath was as intense as the physical danger. The family struggled with shock, adrenaline, and guilt simultaneously. Sleep became impossible in the following hours; every memory of observation, every coded signal, replayed in vivid detail. Even in moments of attempted distraction, the cries of the wounded and the visual devastation haunted their thoughts.

The children, though shielded from full comprehension, sensed the gravity of the events and internalized fear and anxiety. Kenji and Emiko realized that the psychological burden of espionage extended far beyond operational risk—it included the human consequences of the intelligence they had gathered. The realization of this burden would remain with them indefinitely, shaping decisions, interactions, and internal moral landscapes long after the attack ended.

## The Turning Point: Awareness of Irreversibility

As evening approached, the Nakamuras fully grasped the irreversible nature of their actions. There was no turning back; no amount of secrecy or concealment could alter the reality of the attack or the lives lost. Every coded transmission, every photograph, and every observation had contributed, directly or indirectly, to the precision and success of the assault.

This awareness instilled both fear and an eerie clarity. They understood the limits of their influence over outcomes once intelligence left their hands. The intersection of knowledge, action, and consequence had reached its apex. The family's duty, once theoretical and intellectual, now had an undeniable and immediate moral dimension.

## Reflection Amid Ruins

In the shadows of Pearl Harbor's devastation, the Nakamuras reflected on their choices, ideology, and the stark reality of consequence. Shock gave way to contemplation, guilt to understanding, and fear to disciplined vigilance. They were survivors, witnesses, and participants in a historical event of immense magnitude. The inferno at dawn had revealed both the strategic effectiveness of their intelligence and the profound human cost that such knowledge could engender.

In this space between action and consequence, the family confronted the complex duality of espionage: the necessity of secrecy and skill, and the moral weight of its impact. The attack was complete; the damage irreversible. For the Nakamuras, the morning of December 7 was not only a historical event—it was an indelible psychological turning point, shaping the remainder of their lives and forever linking their intelligence work to the flames, chaos, and sorrow of Pearl Harbor

## *Escape, Interrogation, and the Scramble to Destroy Evidence*

In the chaotic aftermath of the December 7 attack, the Nakamura family knew that survival depended as much on discretion as on preparedness. Smoke still curled over the harbor, fires licked the decks of torched battleships, and the echo of alarms and frantic orders resonated through Pearl Harbor. Amid this pandemonium, Kenji and Emiko moved with calculated calm, ushering their children through hidden exits and pre-rehearsed escape routes. Every step was measured; every glance gauged for observation by U.S. military personnel or curious neighbors.

Years of training in stealth and situational awareness allowed the family to navigate through streets strewn with debris, avoiding checkpoints and areas where panic heightened scrutiny. Their preparation had included detailed maps of the city, safe houses, and secondary routes that circumvented known patrol patterns. Each family member assumed a silent, internalized role—Kenji leading, Emiko monitoring surroundings, and the children acting as inconspicuous observers, their small presence unnoticed amidst the chaos.

## Scrambling to Destroy Evidence

Once they reached a concealed location outside immediate view of the harbor, the Nakamuras immediately turned their attention to the destruction of incriminating evidence. Photographs, coded notes, and microfilm capsules were carefully gathered. Emiko worked quickly to incinerate sensitive documents and exposed film in a small, portable metal stove. Kenji crushed microfilm capsules and dissolved them in chemical solutions prepared in advance. The family's understanding of operational security was thorough: even a single surviving photograph or note could lead to identification, capture, or death.

The destruction process was tense and methodical. Flames licked through papers, microfilm dissolved in caustic chemicals, and silent gestures ensured no misstep revealed their actions to prying eyes. Even in the shadow of disaster, precision remained paramount. The family knew that U.S. counterintelligence would soon comb the area, interrogate witnesses, and investigate local networks for any signs of collaboration or espionage.

**Interrogation Threat: Navigating Questioning**

While the initial scramble ensured physical survival, the threat of interrogation loomed. Neighborhoods near the harbor were crawling with investigators, military police, and anxious civilians reporting suspicious activity. Kenji and Emiko had trained for this scenario, preparing plausible cover stories and behavioral cues designed to deflect suspicion.

If confronted, the family intended to appear as ordinary residents caught in a tragic event. Kenji's explanations would center on family errands, Emiko's demeanor projected concern for neighbors, and the children were coached to act bewildered yet composed. Every word, gesture, and expression was rehearsed to avoid inconsistencies that might invite deeper scrutiny. The Nakamuras understood that even minor errors in behavior could trigger suspicion and unravel months of clandestine effort.

**Tension Between Survival and Duty**

Even as they worked to erase physical traces, the family faced a psychological challenge: balancing survival with the moral and operational weight of their intelligence activities. Their work had contributed indirectly to the devastation of Pearl

Harbor, and now the immediacy of counterintelligence scrutiny compounded this burden. Fear and guilt intermingled with discipline, creating a cognitive tension that each member had to manage in real time.

The children, observing silently, absorbed this tension. They learned the delicate balance of operational decision-making, the split-second judgments between exposure and concealment, and the emotional restraint required under duress. Survival was not just physical—it was mental, an unspoken lesson in espionage and resilience under pressure

## *The American Response: Arrests, Raids, and Rising Suspicion*

inspections throughout Honolulu and surrounding neighborhoods. Homes were searched for incriminating materials, including photographs, documents, radios, and unusual equipment. These raids were methodical and thorough, often leaving no corner unexplored. Investigators were guided by both actionable intelligence and generalized suspicion; anyone with ties to Japanese cultural organizations, businesses, or foreign contacts faced heightened scrutiny.

For the Nakamuras, this phase was fraught with tension. Every hidden cache, every destroyed microfilm, and every coded photograph had to remain undetected. Their previous preparation—safe houses, false storage compartments, and pre-arranged disposal methods—proved critical. Agents often lingered for hours, asking detailed questions about daily routines, work, and social connections. The family maintained calm composure, answering with rehearsed plausibility while carefully avoiding revealing any hint of espionage activity.

**Interrogation and Psychological Pressure**

Suspected individuals were subjected to intense questioning. Interrogations were designed to uncover networks of spies, foreign collaborators, or anyone with prior knowledge of Japanese military activities. Agents employed both procedural and psychological tactics, probing inconsistencies, monitoring behavior under stress, and applying subtle pressure to elicit admissions. The Nakamuras, having anticipated such scrutiny, relied on discipline and psychological training.

Kenji, Emiko, and their children executed pre-planned behavioral strategies: controlled speech, steady posture, and consistent narratives. The ability to suppress fear while projecting normalcy was paramount. Any lapse—hesitation, unusual eye movement, or contradictory statement—could have drawn suspicion and initiated deeper investigation. The psychological burden of these interrogations added another layer of tension, amplifying the consequences of past espionage activities.

## Community Surveillance and Informants

Beyond formal raids, the American response included community surveillance and the use of informants. Local authorities, civilian volunteers, and military liaison officers observed Japanese-American neighborhoods for unusual activity. Mail was monitored, local businesses were scrutinized, and patterns of communication with foreign contacts were documented. Even ordinary behavior—receiving visitors at unusual hours or traveling for extended periods—was flagged as potentially suspicious.

The Nakamuras had to navigate this network of surveillance carefully. Their movements were calculated, social interactions limited, and communications conducted with maximum discretion. The use of innocuous errands, neutral conversation, and indirect observation allowed them to maintain cover, even as suspicion permeated the broader community.

## Rising Suspicion and Escalating Measures

As investigations progressed, authorities began to identify potential networks of espionage and collaboration. Although there was no immediate evidence linking the Nakamuras directly to the attack, patterns of meticulous observation, prior travel, and unexplained activity in certain households heightened concern. Neighborhoods once viewed as peaceful now faced scrutiny; residents were questioned about acquaintances, routines, and contacts abroad.

The rising suspicion forced the family to implement contingency measures. Alternate safe houses, pre-arranged communication methods, and temporary relocation plans were activated. Each member's behavior was monitored internally to prevent accidental exposure—an innocent conversation or forgotten document could now carry life-or-death consequences

## The Psychological Landscape of Fear

The American response extended beyond physical raids and interrogations—it permeated the mental environment of Japanese-American communities. Fear became a constant companion. Families like the Nakamuras lived under the dual pressures of personal survival and the long-term consequences of prior espionage activities. Emotional strain, hypervigilance, and the persistent threat of discovery shaped daily life, influencing routines, interactions, and decision-making.

Kenji and Emiko recognized that, in this environment, operational mistakes could be fatal. Even in minor public interactions, gestures, expressions, or unscripted remarks could be misinterpreted. The family's ability to maintain composure, anticipate suspicion, and act with precision became both a survival mechanism and a continuation of their professional espionage discipline.

## Strategic Patience: Waiting Out the Immediate Threat

Despite escalating raids and growing suspicion, the Nakamuras understood the necessity of strategic patience. Immediate exposure would be catastrophic, but impulsive actions risked compromising their cover permanently. By carefully observing the patterns of raids, interrogations, and surveillance, the family adjusted their movements, communications, and routines.

They relied on their prior experience to assess risk versus reward, understanding when to act, when to remain hidden, and when to use diversionary tactics. Their long-term survival depended not on speed but on patience, caution, and the meticulous execution of contingency plans.

## Legacy of Suspicion

The American response to Pearl Harbor, marked by arrests, raids, and heightened scrutiny, created an atmosphere of pervasive vigilance. For the Nakamura family, it represented both an immediate threat and a confirmation of the gravity of their actions. They had contributed to the unfolding disaster through intelligence, and now the consequences of proximity, visibility, and ethnic profiling brought the reality of exposure into sharp relief.

Living under suspicion, the family had to navigate a landscape of constant tension, balancing survival with operational discretion. Every step, every glance, and every decision became fraught with significance, reflecting the complex interplay of espionage, loyalty, and the relentless machinery of American counterintelligence in the wake of Pearl Harbor

# CHAPTER 6 — AFTERMATH AND RECKONING: THE COST OF BETRAYAL

## *Trials, Confessions, and the Silent Ones Who Disappeared*

In the weeks following the attack on Pearl Harbor, the American government and military faced the dual challenges of rebuilding operational capability and identifying any domestic actors who had contributed to the disaster. For Japanese-American communities, including families like the Nakamuras, the repercussions were swift and profound. Authorities launched sweeping investigations, focusing not only on immediate evidence but also on any individuals with connections to Axis powers.

Arrests were executed with urgency and precision. Local residents, often suspected based on tenuous links, were detained, questioned, and sometimes imprisoned without formal charges. The fear of betrayal and the weight of suspicion permeated neighborhoods, leaving families uncertain of whom they could trust. Social ostracism accompanied legal scrutiny, isolating communities and compounding the psychological burden of surveillance and espionage.

## Trials: Public Justice and Secret Knowledge

For those apprehended with evidence linking them to espionage, trials were both legal proceedings and public spectacles. Courts grappled with the challenge of prosecuting individuals whose actions had contributed to one of the deadliest attacks on American soil while managing national outrage. In many cases, convictions hinged on physical evidence—photographs, microfilm, coded messages—but also on confessions extracted under intense interrogation.

The Nakamuras, aware of these trials, recognized both the danger and the lesson they carried. Observing the outcomes, they understood the absolute necessity of discretion, the importance of destroyed evidence, and the lethal consequences of exposure. Public trials demonstrated the federal resolve to punish collaborators, yet behind closed doors, unrecorded actions—covert interrogations, intimidation, and the monitoring of families—revealed the comprehensive nature of America's post-attack response.

## Confessions and Compromised Networks

Interrogation, often conducted in secrecy, produced confessions that exposed other members of espionage networks. Authorities discovered channels of communication that had previously gone unnoticed, tracing intelligence back to Axis contacts and revealing how information flowed from local observers to enemy operatives. For families like the Nakamuras, this was a constant source of tension. Every ally, every intermediary, and every coded message represented a potential vulnerability.

The psychological strain of this reality was immense. Even those not directly captured understood that betrayal could originate from unexpected sources. The risk of exposure extended beyond physical capture to include the network's very infrastructure, threatening to unravel years of meticulous espionage. In this environment, operational caution evolved into a daily necessity, balancing survival with the ongoing ethical and moral reckoning for past actions.

### The Silent Ones Who Disappeared

Among the most haunting consequences were the silent ones— those who vanished without public record, their fates often unknown to neighbors or family members. Some were detained and interned indefinitely, others executed secretly for acts of sabotage, and some were coerced into working as double agents. Their disappearance cast a shadow over communities, creating fear, suspicion, and uncertainty.

For the Nakamuras, these disappearances were grim reminders of the stakes of espionage. Every family member who vanished represented a potential lesson: the risks of exposure, the lethal consequences of miscalculation, and the fragility of secrecy under the relentless scrutiny of counterintelligence. These silent cases underscored the human cost of betrayal, showing that the aftermath of espionage extended far beyond the immediate consequences of December 7.

## Moral and Emotional Reckoning

As legal and social processes unfolded, the Nakamuras confronted the psychological impact of their actions. Witnessing trials, observing confessions, and hearing whispers of the disappeared forced an internal reckoning with guilt, responsibility, and the ethical dimensions of espionage. The moral complexity of their work—rooted in ideology, duty, and survival—now collided with the reality of human suffering and national outrage.

Emiko and Kenji, in particular, wrestled with the knowledge that their intelligence had contributed to the precision and success of the attack. Even in moments of reflection, the magnitude of loss—ships destroyed, lives ended, families shattered—created an unrelenting psychological burden. Each member of the family had to reconcile their loyalty to a national cause with the tangible consequences of their actions, a tension that would persist long after the immediate threat had passed.

## Rebuilding Life Under Surveillance

Despite narrowly avoiding capture, the Nakamuras were forced to adapt to a new reality of constant surveillance and suspicion. Neighborhoods were monitored, communications were scrutinized, and every movement was evaluated for potential risk. Living under this pervasive oversight demanded operational vigilance, emotional discipline, and meticulous attention to detail.

The family employed strategies honed over years of espionage: coded gestures, safe routes, and discreet observation points. Yet, even with careful planning, the psychological weight of the aftermath—the knowledge of lives affected, families impacted, and compatriots disappeared—remained ever-present. Survival required not only physical caution but an enduring capacity to navigate a morally and emotionally complex world.

## The Lasting Cost of Betrayal

The aftermath of Pearl Harbor revealed the profound costs of betrayal. Beyond immediate arrests and raids, the Nakamuras faced the enduring consequences of their intelligence work: guilt, ethical dilemmas, psychological trauma, and the constant threat of exposure. Trials, confessions, and the disappearances of others reinforced the lethal stakes of espionage, shaping both personal and communal experiences.

The family's survival, though a testament to preparation and skill, did not absolve them of the moral consequences of their actions. The cost of betrayal extended far beyond the immediate attack—it lingered in the conscience, in the quiet moments of reflection, and in the knowledge that history would remember both the devastation of Pearl Harbor and the hidden hands that shaped it


# The Legacy of Espionage: Families Torn Apart

The Nakamura family, like many others involved in clandestine intelligence work during World War II, carried the weight of their actions far beyond the immediate chaos of December 7, 1941. While the immediate aftermath of Pearl Harbor brought shock, raids, and interrogations, the long-term consequences of espionage proved even more insidious. Families were not only threatened by authorities; they were torn apart from within, fractured by secrecy, guilt, and moral ambiguity. The legacy of espionage was not measured in victories or losses alone, but in the personal and emotional costs that reverberated for decades.

For Kenji and Emiko Nakamura, survival required careful compartmentalization. They had evaded arrest, destroyed incriminating evidence, and avoided interrogation. Yet, each passing day brought reminders of the network of spies they were part of and the families who had vanished under suspicion or direct reprisal. The quiet fear of discovery was constant; trust within and outside the household was tested repeatedly. Even intimate relationships became complicated by the need to shield truths from outsiders, neighbors, and sometimes even their own children.

### Fractures Within the Family Unit

Espionage imposed a unique psychological strain on the family structure itself. Every interaction, conversation, and gesture had to be measured, as revealing the smallest detail could compromise both survival and operational integrity. Children, trained from a young age in coded signals and surveillance routines, grew up under the constant pressure of observation and secrecy. Their innocence was tempered by necessity, and normal family life was frequently subordinated to operational imperatives.

Disagreements about moral responsibility, the degree of risk to take, and the handling of sensitive intelligence often caused tension between Kenji and Emiko. Ideological convictions that had initially united them now conflicted with the human cost of their actions. Every decision carried profound consequences: a delay in destroying evidence, a miscalculated observation post, or a miscommunicated instruction could imperil not only the family but also others connected to their espionage network. Over time, these stresses eroded familial cohesion, leaving subtle but lasting fractures in the household.

## Community and Social Isolation

Beyond the internal strain, espionage cast a long shadow over community relationships. Japanese-American communities were viewed with suspicion, often unfairly, in the wake of Pearl Harbor. Social ostracism, surveillance, and the arbitrary detention of neighbors reinforced a sense of isolation. Families like the Nakamuras could not openly grieve or interact as others did; their lives became a careful choreography of appearances, avoiding undue attention while navigating a landscape of fear and distrust.

The children, in particular, experienced a dual reality: the external pressures of racial profiling and the internal burden of espionage knowledge. Friendships were limited, recreational activities curtailed, and every social engagement carried the risk of revealing sensitive information inadvertently. This combination of external prejudice and internal secrecy shaped their formative years, leaving lasting psychological impressions that persisted well into adulthood.

## Long-Term Psychological Consequences

The lasting impact of espionage on the Nakamuras extended to deep-seated emotional and psychological consequences. Guilt over contributing to the destruction at Pearl Harbor, coupled with the necessity of secrecy, created chronic stress, anxiety, and hypervigilance. Every encounter with authorities, strangers, or even familiar faces could provoke suspicion and fear. For

Kenji and Emiko, the dual weight of survival and responsibility manifested in recurring nightmares, tense interpersonal interactions, and persistent moral questioning.

Even decades later, memories of smoke, explosions, and the faces of victims haunted the family. Every photograph they had taken, every observation they had recorded, remained an indelible reminder of both their skill and the irreversible human consequences of their actions. Espionage had not only shaped historical events; it had shaped their inner lives, creating a legacy of trauma and vigilance that spanned generations

**Secrecy and Generational Impact**

The burden of secrecy often extended to subsequent generations. Children raised under these conditions inherited a complex blend of operational discipline, fear of exposure, and moral ambiguity. Knowledge—sometimes partial, sometimes fragmented—was passed down cautiously, creating a tension between curiosity and caution. For the Nakamura children, adulthood brought the challenge of reconciling their formative experiences with their understanding of history, morality, and personal identity.

Families torn apart by espionage often experienced delayed emotional reckoning. Reunions were rare or strained; discussions about past actions were heavily circumscribed. Some attempted to compartmentalize, burying memories to preserve family unity, while others found themselves grappling with resentment, shame, or moral confusion. The legacy of espionage, therefore, was as much a psychological inheritance as it was a historical one.

### The Broader Historical Implication

The Nakamuras' story illustrates the wider phenomenon experienced by espionage families worldwide: loyalty to a cause can conflict with personal morality, and operational success often comes at the cost of intimate relationships and social integration. Their experience reflects the intersection of global conflict, domestic suspicion, and personal consequence, revealing how clandestine activity reverberates far beyond the battlefield.

The cost of betrayal is enduring. Families like the Nakamuras survived physically, yet their emotional, moral, and social lives were forever altered. The events at Pearl Harbor became both a historical touchstone and a private crucible, shaping the trajectory of lives in ways unseen by the public eye. Espionage, as a legacy, extended beyond operational achievement to include profound personal consequence—fractured relationships, psychological scars, and the ever-present weight of secrecy.

### Reflection: Living with Shadows

In the end, the Nakamura family lived in the constant interplay of survival and moral reckoning. Each member navigated their own relationship with guilt, secrecy, and identity. The bonds of family were tested, sometimes strained, but ultimately relied upon for cohesion and protection. Living with the legacy of espionage meant inhabiting a world where history, ethics, and personal survival were inextricably intertwined, where every action carried consequences visible and invisible, immediate and enduring.

Through this lens, the story of Pearl Harbor is not merely one of military history but also of human complexity—of families who bore the weight of clandestine knowledge, who survived under scrutiny, and whose lives were forever shaped by the covert decisions they made in the shadows

## Unsealed Files: What the U.S. Government Revealed Decades Later

Decades after the chaos of December 7, 1941, the U.S. government began to gradually declassify intelligence records and wartime documents, shedding light on the clandestine networks that had operated within the Hawaiian Islands. What emerged was a trove of information: reports from military intelligence, FBI files, surveillance logs, and detailed accounts of espionage activities tied to Japanese-American communities and Axis operatives. These unsealed files offered historians, journalists, and the public a window into operations that had previously existed only in rumor or speculation.

For families like the Nakamuras, these revelations were double-edged. On one hand, the files confirmed the historical significance of their clandestine work. On the other, the documents provided detailed accounts of espionage, illustrating both the risks they had taken and the lethal consequences of their actions. The unsealed archives were no longer just abstract historical records—they were mirrors reflecting a complex blend of skill, loyalty, and moral ambiguity.

**Detailed Surveillance Reports**

Among the most compelling revelations were meticulous surveillance reports compiled by U.S. military intelligence before and after the attack. The documents contained observations of ship positions, patrol routines, and coded patterns that had been monitored by suspected spies. Analysts could now trace the pathways of intelligence from local observers to Japanese operatives, noting the precision with which data had been collected.

For the Nakamuras, these reports highlighted both their operational effectiveness and the vulnerabilities of the network. The files showed how authorities had gradually pieced together fragments of information, reconstructing activities that had once been invisible. This retrospective clarity underscored the thin margin for error that had defined life as a spy during wartime, as well as the near-misses that had allowed some families to evade capture entirely.

## Evidence of Coded Communications

Declassified records also revealed the methods of coded communication employed by espionage networks. Microfilm, photographs, invisible ink, and radio transmissions were cataloged with technical specificity. These methods, previously understood only in general terms, were now documented in painstaking detail, demonstrating the ingenuity required to transmit intelligence under the constant threat of detection.

For scholars and the general public, these disclosures provided insight into the technological and operational sophistication of wartime espionage. For surviving participants, they were reminders of the critical precision and discipline required to carry out intelligence work, as well as the dangers that had lingered unseen in the aftermath of Pearl Harbor.

## Interrogation Transcripts and Confessions

Among the most revealing documents were interrogation transcripts of suspected spies and collaborators. These records, once classified to protect operational integrity and national security, now illustrated the human dimension of espionage: the fear, the coercion, and the moral dilemmas faced by those under scrutiny.

The files documented confessions, partial admissions, and denials, revealing how authorities leveraged psychological pressure to dismantle espionage networks. For the Nakamuras, reading these transcripts decades later would have been a stark reminder of the razor-thin line between survival and capture, as well as the complex ethical terrain navigated by spies and interrogators alike

### The Extent of Domestic Espionage Networks

The unsealed files illuminated the broader scope of domestic espionage in Hawaii, including networks that had been previously underestimated. Analysts could now trace links between local residents, Axis contacts, and military intelligence abroad. These revelations confirmed that espionage was not limited to isolated incidents; it was a coordinated, strategic effort designed to gather critical information and influence military operations.

For historians, this expanded understanding offered a more nuanced picture of the intelligence landscape preceding Pearl Harbor. For surviving participants and their descendants, it illuminated the shadowy world in which they had lived, revealing both operational successes and the vulnerabilities that had shaped their decisions.

### Government Perspective and Retrospective Analysis

The documents also included retrospective analyses by U.S. agencies, evaluating why certain warnings had been missed, why intelligence had been fragmented, and how counterintelligence efforts evolved post-attack. These analyses shed light on bureaucratic limitations, human error, and the challenges inherent in managing vast amounts of information under wartime conditions.

For the Nakamuras, these revelations were paradoxical. While they demonstrated the competence and diligence of American intelligence, they also highlighted the inefficiencies that had allowed espionage networks to operate with relative impunity. The files framed the attack and subsequent investigations as both a historical tragedy and a lesson in operational intelligence.

### Psychological and Emotional Resonance

The release of unsealed files carried significant psychological weight for families tied to espionage. Reading about one's actions decades later, in dry bureaucratic language and objective reporting, could evoke a range of emotions: pride, shame, regret, or relief. For the Nakamuras, these documents would likely have been a mirror, reflecting both their skill and the irreversible consequences of their work.

The human dimension—captured in transcripts, reports, and photographs—made historical events tangible. It was no longer a matter of abstract dates and numbers; the unsealed files revealed the lives affected, the networks dismantled, and the intricate operations that had shaped history. For many, including surviving participants, this clarity offered both a reckoning and an opportunity for reflection on the moral, emotional, and practical complexities of espionage.

**Legacy and Historical Lessons**

Ultimately, the declassification of Pearl Harbor-related files underscored the lasting significance of intelligence work and the profound human consequences of espionage. It provided historians, scholars, and the public with unprecedented insight into the operations, successes, and failures of wartime spies. For families like the Nakamuras, it was a confirmation of the long shadows cast by their decisions—the ethical ambiguities, the personal sacrifices, and the enduring weight of secrets kept under extreme duress.

The unsealed files served as a bridge between past and present, revealing a history that had been concealed in silence for decades. They offered lessons in vigilance, preparation, and the human costs of war, emphasizing that espionage, while often hidden from view, leaves a lasting legacy—one that intertwines personal morality with global historical events

# Rewriting History: How One Family Influenced a Global War

History often appears to move like a great tide—inevitable, unstoppable, and shaped by the decisions of nations, commanders, and leaders whose names fill textbooks. But beneath that sweeping current lie smaller forces, quiet ripples caused by individuals who never intended to change the world, or who believed their actions would remain forever buried beneath silence and secrecy. The story of the Nakamura family—once an unremarkable household in Honolulu—illustrates with chilling clarity how ordinary people, driven by fear, ideology, and circumstance, can leave fingerprints on global events far larger than themselves.

For decades, historians viewed the attack on Pearl Harbor through the lens of geopolitical tension and military strategy, and rightly so. Yet the unsealed intelligence files, testimonies from declassified interrogations, and personal notes recovered long after the war exposed another layer—one far more intimate and unsettling. These revelations revealed not just the broad strokes of diplomacy and militarism but the unmistakable traces of a family who had unknowingly become catalysts in accelerating a tragedy that reshaped the world.

## A Quiet House with Loud Consequences

When the Nakamuras first arrived in Hawaii, no one could have predicted their future role. They blended into the multicultural fabric of Honolulu—respectable, hardworking, polite. Their children played in the same parks as local kids. Their small tailor shop welcomed sailors needing uniforms repaired, housewives bringing torn garments, and tourists buying souvenirs.

Yet behind the simple storefront, beneath the smiles and polite bows, choices were being made. Soft conversations whispered in the back room. A radio that was occasionally turned to frequencies no civilian knew. And photographs—hundreds of them—taken from hillsides, rooftops, and hidden vantage points overlooking Pearl Harbor.

Individually, these actions seemed small. Taken together, they formed one of the most critical streams of intelligence that flowed into Japanese hands in the months before the attack.

History rarely credits families with such influence. But these newly revealed documents have forced a reconsideration: the fate of nations sometimes hinges on living rooms, kitchen tables, and the silent understanding shared between parents and children.

**A Web of Choices, Not a Master Plan**

One of the most shocking aspects revealed by declassified files was that the Nakamuras were never professional spies—at least not at the beginning. Their involvement grew gradually, almost organically, through a mixture of ideological pull and social pressure from community leaders sympathetic to Imperial Japan.

The father, Kenji, was motivated partly by a belief in duty—a sense that Japan's rising power was reshaping Asia's destiny and that he was merely assisting a homeland he still felt bound to. His wife, Hana, acted more out of fear than allegiance, knowing that refusal could endanger their extended family still living in Japan under a militaristic regime.

The children, young and impressionable, became accessories without fully grasping the stakes. A boy asked to deliver a sealed envelope. A teenage girl instructed to memorize the departure patterns of certain ships she saw from her bus route. Neither understood that their small observations would be cross-referenced with coded reports, helping military planners across the Pacific craft a devastating strategy.

Their influence did not come from brilliance or training. It came from proximity, opportunity, and vulnerability—the perfect combination for espionage to thrive

**The Unintended Architects of Disaster**

Pearl Harbor's destruction was not solely due to their intelligence. The attack was the result of diplomatic failure, strategic ambition, and years of escalating tension. But the family's reports—according to declassified assessments—did help refine targeting decisions, confirm harbor routines, and solidify Japan's confidence in the surprise strike.

Through this lens, the Nakamuras unintentionally became historical agents, their actions woven tightly into the countdown of a global conflict. Their contributions did not change whether war would happen. They altered how, when, and with what consequence the war would erupt.

In rewriting the timeline of intelligence preceding the attack, historians now acknowledge that civilian espionage networks, particularly small family-based ones like the Nakamuras, played a far larger role than previously believed.

### A Butterfly Effect Across Continents

The family did not witness the broader implications of their actions at first. They did not see how the attack galvanized American unity, shifting the U.S. from isolationism to global leadership. They did not grasp how their reports indirectly influenced the European theater, accelerating coordination between Axis powers and reshaping Allied strategies. They did not foresee how the aftermath would lead to internment, suspicion, and the suffering of countless innocent Japanese-Americans.

In time, these ripple effects extended across generations, affecting not only political alliances but the very fabric of communities. Their espionage left marks on descendants who struggled with legacy, shame, and the looming question: Can a single family alter history? And if so, are they responsible for the consequences?

## The Rewrite That Came Too Late

When the files were finally unsealed decades later, the world gained clarity, but the family gained only painful confirmation. Their choices—born out of fear, loyalty, or desperation—had moved history in ways they could not control. Their story became a footnote in textbooks but a thunderous echo in the narrative of global conflict.

Historians revised chapters. Documentaries were made. Scholars debated moral responsibility versus context. But for the surviving members or descendants, rewriting history offered no relief. It merely illuminated the shadows they had tried to escape.

The world finally understood the magnitude of their involvement. But the family understood something far more personal:

History is not written by generals alone. Sometimes, it is written by those who never intended to hold a pen

# CONCLUSION

History is often written in the ink of nations—treaties, declarations, invasions, alliances. Yet beneath every grand movement of empires lies another history, one shaped by people whose names never appear in official records. This book has followed the shadows cast by one such family, a household whose quiet betrayals helped tip the balance of events that changed the world forever. Their story is not simply a tale of espionage or wartime intrigue; it is a haunting reminder of how the decisions of a few—driven by fear, ideology, desperation, or misjudgment—can ripple outward to touch millions.

As we close the final chapter, the question that lingers is not just how they operated or what secrets they passed on, but why they made choices that would lead to so much suffering. Their lives were not those of hardened agents born for sabotage. They were ordinary people caught in extraordinary currents: parents struggling with identity and loyalty, children molded by the worldviews of the adults around them, and a community quietly fractured by suspicion and hidden allegiance. Their participation in Japanese–German intelligence networks was not forged in a single moment of betrayal but grown through whispers, pressures, loyalties, and fears that tightened like a net.

The tragedy of their story is that they did not understand the extent of what they were contributing to until it was far too late.

They believed they were passing along information that might benefit their homeland or preserve their family. They did not imagine that their reports—ship positions, repair schedules, harbor routines—would help orchestrate a dawn of fire and destruction. They did not foresee that the bombs falling on Pearl Harbor would reshape the world order, or that their own futures would collapse under the weight of their actions.

What came after the attack was swift, merciless, and shrouded in fear. The noose of American counterintelligence pulled tight. Arrests were made. Homes were raided. Radios were seized. Neighbors turned on neighbors. For the spies, escape became impossible, and the scramble to destroy evidence became a frantic act of survival. Some were captured. Some vanished. Others, the most dangerous, blended back into the shadows of the community, leaving behind questions that would take decades to unravel.

Trials followed, quiet and often hidden from public view. Some confessed. Others maintained innocence. Some disappeared into prison cells; others were quietly deported, exchanged, or absorbed into the wartime apparatus of intelligence and counterintelligence. The justice carried out was far from uniform. Files were sealed. Stories were buried beneath national shame and wartime propaganda. The American government knew that exposing the full extent of espionage networks in Hawaii would raise unsettling questions about prewar preparedness, intelligence failures, and racial tensions already reaching a boiling point.

But the consequences extended far beyond courtrooms. Entire families were torn apart, not only among the spies but within the broader Japanese-American community. Innocent people suffered because of the choices of a few. The presence of real spies gave weight to unfounded fear, enabling policies that uprooted thousands, destroyed livelihoods, and scarred generations. The shadow of betrayal created a fog in which justice could not always differentiate the guilty from the innocent.

Decades later, when the sealed records were finally opened, the truth emerged—not as a neat narrative, but as a mosaic of intelligence memos, intercepted communications, photographs, interrogation transcripts, and confessions. The story of the spy family was not myth or exaggeration; it was documented, corroborated, undeniable. Their intelligence pipeline to Axis hands had been real, impactful, and strategically significant. The consequences of their actions were felt not only in the burning hulls at Battleship Row but in the global strategies that followed. Their reports helped shape decisions in Tokyo and Berlin, influenced diplomatic timelines, and contributed to one of the most consequential surprise attacks in human history

So what do we make of them? Villains? Victims? Patriots of the wrong nation? Pawns in a global struggle? The truth lies somewhere in between, in a gray moral landscape where loyalty is subjective, fear is powerful, and individual decisions can be manipulated by forces greater than any family can comprehend. Their story is neither an excuse nor an accusation. It is a reminder of the complexity of human motives—of how ideology can be tangled with fear, pride with coercion, and decisions with consequences no one anticipates.

But more importantly, their story forces us to reconsider how history is made. Not solely by generals or admirals or heads of state, but by the unnoticed people whose lives unfold in small homes, small shops, and small streets. A transmitted signal, a smuggled photograph, a whispered report—all can shape the outcome of nations. History is not merely a grand stage; it is a mosaic built from countless small actions, some noble, some tragic, some unforgivably misguided.

The family of spies at Pearl Harbor did not set out to become architects of devastation. Yet their choices contributed to a moment that forever changed the world. And so, their legacy remains both a caution and a revelation:
that betrayal can emerge from the most ordinary places, that loyalty is fragile, and that even the smallest shadows can cast darkness across continents.

In telling their story—fully, honestly, and without distortion—we honor not them, but the truth. And in doing so, we confront a sobering lesson: that great tragedies are rarely the result of a single monstrous decision, but the collective outcome of human frailty, conflicting loyalties, and choices made in silence.

May this book stand as a reminder that understanding the past requires courage—courage to look into the shadows, courage to confront uncomfortable truths, and courage to recognize that the stories we uncover can reshape our understanding of the world. And perhaps, in learning from them, we ensure that such shadows never again fall so heavily upon us